CW00832056

The Healing Power
of Sufi Meditation

Published by
Naqshbandi Haqqani Sufi Order of America

HAQQANI

© Copyright 2005 by the Naqshbandi Haqqani Sufi Order of America. All rights reserved.
ISBN: 1-930409-26-5

No part of this book may be reproduced, stored in a retrieval system, or transmitted in any form, or by any means, electronic, mechanical, photocopying, or otherwise, without the written permission of the Naqshbandi Haqqani Sufi Order of America.

Library of Congress Cataloging-in-Publication Data

Mirahmadi, As-Sayyid Nurjan and Mirahmadi, Hedieh Dr.
  The healing power of Sufi meditation and divine energy / by As-Sayyid Nurjan Mirahmadi and Hedieh Mirahmadi from the teachings of Shaykh Muhammad Nazim Adil al-Haqqani as passed to his deputy, Shaykh Muhammad Hisham Kabbani; foreword by Shaykh Muhammad Nazim Adil al-Haqqani; introduction by Shaykh Muhammad Hisham Kabbani.
     p. cm.
  Includes bibliographical references.
  ISBN 1-930409-26-5
  1. Naqshabandeiyah--Prayer-books and devotions. 2. Sufism--Prayer-books and devotions. 3. Sufi chants. 4. Spiritual healing. I. al-Haqqani, Shaykh Muhammad Nazim Adil II. Kabbani, Shaykh Muhammad Hisham. III. Mirahmadi, Hedieh. IV. Mirahmadi, as-Sayyid Nurjan
  BP189.7.N35M57 2005
  297.4'382--dc22
                                    2005001975

Illustrations by Salim Djebili
Book Cover and Graphic Design by Christina Matsoukis

Published and Distributed by:
Naqshbandi Haqqani Sufi Order of America
17195 Silver Parkway, #206
Fenton, MI 48430 USA
Tel: (810) 593-1222 Fax: (810) 815-0518
Email: staff@naqshbandi.org, staff@nurmuhammad.com
Web: www.naqshbandi.org, www.nurmuhammad.com

The Healing Power of Sufi Meditation

by
as-Sayyid Nurjan Mirahmadi
& Hedieh Mirahmadi

Foreword by Shaykh Muhammad Adil Nazim al-Haqqani
Introduction by Shaykh Muhammad Hisham Kabbani

Table of Contents

Chapter 2
Divine Energy

Chapter 3
Angelic Healing

Picture Gallery

Shaykh Muhammad Nazim Adil al-Haqqani (pictured upper right) is the author of this book's foreword and is the world leader of the Naqshbandi Haqqani Sufi Order. Shaykh Muhammad Hisham Kabbani (pictured upper left and lower left) is the author of this book's introduction and deputy leader of the Order. Together the two Shaykh's hold the love and respect of millions around the world. Shaykh Adnan Kabbani is Shaykh Muhammad Hisham Kabbani's brother and is pictured on the lower right.

Hedieh Mirahmadi and as-Sayyid Nurjan Mirahmadi, co-authors of this book.

Shaykh Sharif of Holland.

*Shaykh Muhammad Hisham
Kabbani & His Royal Highness
Raja Ashman Shah Ibni Sultan
Azlan Shah, Prince of Perak,
Malaysia.*

*Shaykh Lutfi (left) and Shaykh
Moustafa of Indonesia(right).*

*Shaykh Hassan of Germany
demonstrating Sufi Meditation
technique.*

*Shaykh Muhammad Nazim
Adil al-Haqqani and Shaykh
Yusuf Da Costa of South
Africa.*

Shaykh Jamaluddin of Germany.

*Shaykh Omar Margarit of Spain (left)
with Shaykh Muhammad Hisham
Kabbani (right).*

Preface

*T*his book is based on the teachings of Shaykh Muhammad Nazim Adil al-Haqqani, world leader of the Naqshbandi-Haqqani Sufi Order, who passed this ancient wisdom to his deputy, Shaykh Muhammad Hisham Kabbani. Shaykh Kabbani is in charge of disseminating the spiritual knowledge of Mawlana Shaykh Nazim Adil al-Haqqani internationally and especially in America. Together the shaykhs hold the love and attention of millions of followers around the world.

The teachings are presented in this book by as-Sayyid Nurjan Mirahmadi and Dr. Hedieh Mirahmadi, who are authorized to speak on behalf of Shaykh Hisham and are experts in the Sufi science of meditation known as *muraqabah*.

The book is a *how-to guide* whereby the student gains access to communications from the heart of the Sufi spiritual guide, which can only be achieved through meditation and contemplation.

This book is designed to be accessible to non-Muslims and thus we have taken out superfluous Arabic words and the original Arabic Quranic and hadith (traditions of the Prophet Muhammad ﷺ) language, leaving only the English translation. Some limited use of Arabic words remains – for instance "*Sayyidina*" for "Our master" and other terms deemed essential to the understanding of this technical topic. The invocations of blessings also remain in the text following the names of holy people. Prayers that must be said in Arabic in order to have their full effect are left in Arabic, but are also translated into English. Where Arabic words are important to and explained by the substance of the text, they have been left.

For people knowledgeable about Arabic and Islam: we apologize for the vastly simplified transliteration style used in the body of this book (we have included diacritic marks only in the prayer instructions in the

Appendix). Our experience has been that: (1) people insist that the level of accuracy of transliteration at least match their own knowledge of Arabic; and (2) transliteration symbols, when unfamiliar, make for heavy and difficult reading. Since this book is designed to be inviting and accessible to people with no knowledge of Arabic or Islam, we have completely omitted the diacritic marks. We ask for your patience with this uneasy compromise between accuracy and accessibility.

Traditions of the Prophet Muhammad ﷺ have been placed in the text but without full chains of transmission. The traditions included in this book are firmly established and should be familiar to and immediately accepted on sight by the vast majority of Muslims and certainly scholars.

We use the personal pronouns "he" and "him" when speaking about a person who may be male or female—"he" is less awkward than the other solutions to this problem. We do not wish to offend women who read the book; this decision is only to improve flow.

We welcome any comments, suggestions or criticisms; please direct any correspondence to the address on the copyright page of this book.

Acknowledgements

We never could have quenched our thirst for spiritual enlightenment without the fountain of Divine guidance and inspiration that gushes forth from His Holiness Mawlana Shaykh Nazim Adil al-Haqqani. We owe him an eternity of gratitude for taking us from the "darkness into the light." We are especially grateful that he graced us with his beloved student and deputy, Shaykh Muhammad Hisham Kabbani, as a living example of Sufi chivalry, from whom we could learn and aspire to emulate.

Our profound gratitude also goes out to Hajjah Naziha Adil Kabbani for her boundless patience and selfless generosity. We also would like to thank the countless hours of editing and refinement done by the other students, especially Jamaluddin Hoffman and Mateen Siddiqui, as well as the wonderful illustrations provided by Salim Grant.

We dedicate this book in loving memory of our holy mother, Hajjah Amina Adil. She was the perfect example of spirituality, devotion, and kindness. Her presence is dearly missed.

About the Authors

as-Sayyid Nurjan Mirahmadi

*H*aving achieved business success at a remarkably young age, Shaykh Mirahmadi retired to pursue his religious studies and devote himself to the service of the needy. He then founded an international relief organization, a spiritual healing center and a religious social group for at-risk youth.

In 1995, he became a protégé of Shaykh Muhammad Hisham Kabbani for in-depth studies in Islamic spirituality known as Sufism. Together with Shaykh Kabbani, he has established a number of other Islamic educational organizations and relief programs throughout the world.

He has traveled extensively throughout the world learning and teaching Sufi meditation and healing, understanding the channeling of Divine energy, discipline of the self, and the process of self-realization. He teaches these spiritual arts to groups around the world, regardless of religious denomination.

as-Sayyid Nurjan has six wonderful children and a loving wife, Colette, who has been his partner and reservoir of emotional support throughout this journey.

Dr. Hedieh Mirahmadi

Dr. Mirahmadi was raised in Southern California where she received her law degree from UCLA. A deeply spiritual person, Dr. Mirahmadi turned to the study of the Sufi path after a series of personal events focused her on the need for self-realization. Transforming the direction of her life, Dr. Mirahmadi quickly realized that in a world wrought with hatred, fear and conflict, Sufi meditation could take practitioners to an ethereal place outside their minds within their subconscious where they were free to encounter the healing power of divine energy.

Dr. Mirahmadi went on to direct the Islamic Supreme Council of America, teaching Muslim communities around the world how to create vibrant civil society infrastructure, such as setting up community centers, orphanages, clinics, youth hostels and boarding schools where people could meet in harmony and peace.

Dr Mirahmadi's latest endeavor is her most significant, both personally and in the long term challenge of bringing freedom to areas overrun by rampant corruption and tyranny. As Executive Director and founder of the WORDE (World Organization for Research, Development and Education), Dr. Mirahmadi has combined her political, social and intellectual savvy of the Muslim world to create the policy and networks that will transform stifled and oppressed Muslim communities into progressive, self-sustaining, institutions of grass roots democracy.

Foreword

by Shaykh Muhammad Nazim Adil al-Haqqani

*M*uraqabah is meditation. Meditation is concentration and focus. Meditation is to ask and to find a way to reach for what you are seeking. It is the last level, the last point, that our spirituality reaches. Meditation is not sitting on your legs, crossing your legs, closing your eyes and thinking that you are reaching what you are seeking. This is only imitation, not meditation.

Meditation is not for beginners. It is the last level for the travelers of this Way, the highest level of Sufi practice. Meditation is not for everyone. The beginner must first be prepared and trained through other spiritual practices that lead to the development of the characteristics necessary to reach the level of meditation. He must learn the rules and master the methodology of Sufism to reach that point. He must be trained.

This training is essential, because meditation requires you to stop some of your feelings and desires. You must eliminate them to prepare for even the first step of meditation. You are filled with useless things and must purify yourself and learn to control these thoughts and feelings before your practice of Sufi meditation can be successful. Sufi meditation is a connection, and your physical being must be able to carry that connection. If you meditate and yet remain under the control of your physical desires, then your meditation will be false. You may believe that you are meditating, but you will only be deluding yourself. You cannot succeed in this discipline without first purifying yourself and learning how to block such distractions. In Sufi meditation, you must drop everything from your desires except for the love of that one

1

upon whom you are meditating. You must break every desire except the love of that one. If other desires remain, then your meditation will be fruitless. You may claim that you are practicing meditation, but there will be no basis for that claim.

Just as a river that runs to the ocean upon reaching it becomes one with it, so does the path of Sufi meditation lead the seeker to annihilation in that which he is seeking. However, this requires the seeker to maintain a single-minded focus upon his goal. Only if he is willing and able to leave everything and turn inward with undivided attention can he travel this path to its end. If he does, then he will find what he is seeking.

Sufi Meditation with the Spiritual Master

You may make Sufi meditation to the spiritual master (Shaykh). Consider the Prophetic tradition that states:

> Without a doubt, knowledge is acquired by learning, and forbearance is acquired by demonstrating forbearance.

We are not putting the guide in the heavens nor putting him beside the Holy Throne. We are not making meditation to the shaykh, imagining he is sitting on the Throne. We are not saying this at all. We are speaking of the material world. To make meditation to the guide, the spiritual master, is to listen, to hear, and to accept clearly what the shaykh is teaching you. Meditation to the master is to be in the Presence of the Shaykh (*huduru 'sh-shaykh*) That is Sufi meditation. If he is not there, there is no Sufi meditation. Real Sufi meditation is for God, but the master is preparing you to reach the Divine Presence and to make true Sufi meditation.

It is like the construction of a rocket. The scientists, engineers and technicians prepare everything. They put the crew on board and launch the spacecraft. However, those scientists, engineers and technicians who are on Earth must first prepare the atmosphere on the spacecraft for those who want to reach the moon, or Mars, or Venus, or Pluto, or Neptune, or Jupiter or wherever. They do this while they are still on Earth. In the same way, the Sufi guide is preparing his followers and sending them on to the Divine Presence. The shaykh is not saying, "Connect to me instead of your Lord, and be with me." No! He is only preparing you.

As we mentioned, the Prophet ﷺ said:

Without a doubt, knowledge is [acquired] by learning.

A person who is asking to reach the station of meditation with their Lord must first be prepared. The master teaches his students how they must be in order to be ready to reach their Lord's meditation. He does this through Sufi meditation. Whether his disciples are near or far, the master prepares them through Sufi meditation, just as engineers prepare a rocket for its ascent. Through Sufi meditation, the shaykh is teaching a way of making meditation to God. Before you can reach the Divine Presence, your heart must be with the shaykh and your mind must be with the shaykh's mind, so that you will be prepared. You cannot prepare yourself, by yourself, for such a journey.

Consider the Prophet's ﷺ Night Journey. Even he first had to prepare. He did not go directly up to the heavens. First, the archangels Israfil ﷺ, Michael ﷺ and Gabriel ﷺ came to him in the Sacred Mosque.[1]

They were preparing the Prophet ﷺ for meditation with his Lord Almighty, and they did not leave him until he was ready. Archangel Gabriel ﷺ brought him to the Station of the Highest Lote Tree.[2] Up to that point, he was in meditation with Archangel Gabriel ﷺ. When they reached that station, then Archangel Gabriel ﷺ left, saying, "My meditation is finished. *Muraqabah* with me is finished. Now you have reached what you were asking for." Archangel Gabriel ﷺ could not pass that point because that is the boundary beyond which the mind can no longer function, beyond which there can be no understanding.

Those who have the requisite spiritual abilities can bring to mind the inheritors of the Prophet ﷺ, in order that they may prepare them for the journey to the Divine Presence. They may use their imagination to bring the spiritual master to mind, but it requires special power. Sometimes, the shaykh will appear to them through dreams. Sometimes, if the seeker is more advanced, they may look for the shaykh while they are awake and find him. The spiritual guide is a means. He is not the target. The guide is serving, helping and directing his disciple. Therefore, the disciple must be with the guide. He must make meditation with his master.

The shaykh is looking after his disciple, and through Sufi meditation, he may correct any wrong actions of his disciple. Just as a driving school instructor teaches new drivers to prepare them for their licenses, the shaykh instructs his students to prepare them for the journey to the Divine Presence. In driver's training, the instructor sits next to the student and looks after him, seeing how he is doing. If he is not looking, the student may have an accident. Therefore, the teacher is sitting next to him and teaching him. When he learns, then he receives his license and there is no longer a need for the instructor to be always with him.

---

[1] The Sacred Mosque in Makkah.

[2] *sidratu 'l-muntaha*: the Lote-tree of the Farthest Limit, the station beyond which archangel Gabriel ﷺ could not go, but which Prophet Muhammad ﷺ surpassed on the Night Journey to the Divine Presence.

SUFI MEDITATION AND THE SUFI BOND

Meditation, or *muraqabah*, is different from the Sufi bond (*rabitah*). The Sufi bond is not meditation. God said:

O ye who believe! Persevere in patience and constancy;
vie in such perseverance; strengthen each other (rabitu);
and fear God that ye may prosper. (3:200)

This means you must tie yourself to your spiritual master. This is what you do when you are initiated into this Order, when you take initiation (*baya'*) with your guide. *Rabitah* means "to be bound." If you are not bound, you will be lost. Initiation is establishing the bond. Everyone who is initiated is bound to the guide. Thus, he may be representing thousands or millions of disciples, just as the Prophet Muhammad ﷺ is representing his entire Nation in the Divine Presence.

When you establish the bond, you reaffirm this connection. You say, "I am under my guide's control. I am under his dominion." Everyone that has a guide is under his dominion. You must *feel* that you are under his dominion. Dominion means accepting one's spiritual master will never leave him to succumb to any evil or devils. Dominion is the power of spiritual masters. You must know that you are in his dominion, in his authorized area. You must say, "I am swimming, trying to reach the beach of his dominion, to find the way towards my Lord."

THE METHODOLOGY OF SUFI MEDITATION

The best time for Sufi meditation is during the last half of the night. The seeker must sit down and must try to forget everything in existence except their guides, asking to reach the Divine Presence.

When you make Sufi meditation, you must close your eyes, so as not to be distracted by things that are around you. It is best to perform Sufi meditation in the dark, because this helps the seeker blot everything else out of existence, leaving him alone with his Lord, Almighty God, alone with the Prophet ﷺ and alone with his spiritual guide.

The Lord Almighty, Exalted and Glorified, said to the Prophet Adam ﷺ:

I am going to send to you My Guidance." (2:38)

The word used here for "guidance" is *huda,* an adjective. In this sense, guidance must be dressed on a person so that they can follow it and benefit from it. Therefore, when God is saying, "I am sending to you My Guidance," it means He is sending some specially prepared and trained minds who know, so that the children of Adam ﷺ might be led to the Truth.

God is saying to us, "You cannot reach Me except through following My Guidance." Initially, that guidance came from the prophets, may God's blessing be upon them all. After the prophets, their inheritors have continued to provide this guidance to humanity. If you want to be a guide, then you must be dressed with guidance. Those who seek this must follow the inheritors of the Prophet ﷺ. They must live with them. They must sacrifice themselves to be with them in their ocean of understanding. This, then, is Sufi meditation—to throw your self through that one's real being to reach the guide's reality. Where your guide is going, you must follow. You must be with him. That is Sufi meditation.

God said:

> *And if, as is sure, there comes to you Guidance from me, whosoever follows My guidance, on them shall be no fear, nor shall they grieve. (2:38)*

You must follow your guide step-by-step, so that no devil can come between you and your guide. In this way, you accompany your guide (*murafaqah*), just as the Companions (*Sahaba*) did with the Prophet ☸. The Companions made meditation with the Prophet ☸. The Prophet's ☸ whole will was with meditation. Without meditation, you cannot follow guidance. Those who say otherwise are wrong; this is clear proof.

Everyone has a spirituality in which they have been dressed, and our spirituality is according to our belief power. The Prophet's ☸ spirituality must cover his Nation, reaching everybody who believes in him. Sufi guides also have a very powerful attraction, in order to make it desirable for people to follow them. This attraction is a form of spiritual gravity, majesty. The spiritual guide must have some special characteristics, because their spirituality may affect the personalities of their followers.

ANSWERING THOSE WHO REJECT MEDITATION

Today, there are some who say that making meditation to the Sufi guide is a form of polytheism.[3] Are they saying that a servant must relate directly to the Divine Presence by himself? If they are saying this, that means they are denying the use of a means[4] or vehicle,[5] which has always been a central element of Islamic spirituality. In this sense, it is certainly permitted.

When a traveler needs to reach his homeland, he needs a vehicle. Without a vehicle, he cannot reach his destination. The same is true for the spiritual traveler. He, too, needs a vehicle – in this case, a spiritual one. God referred to this in the Holy Qur'an, when He said:

O ye who believe! Do your duty to God, seek the means of approach unto Him (5: 35)

Thus, God orders the seeker to find a means to Him. In the same way, those who wish to speak to the Prophet ﷺ—to reach the Prophetic Presence—must likewise use a vehicle.

The permitted is clear and the forbidden is clear,[6] according to the Tradition (*hadith*) of the Prophet ﷺ. People cannot declare something forbidden just because they do not understand it. However, some people are always declaring things to be polytheism. In doing so, they are giving themselves the value of polytheism, because they are giving themselves the authority to make something permissible or forbidden.

What, then, is their proof that meditation is forbidden? You cannot find any verse in the Holy Qur'an or the Traditions of the Prophet ﷺ

---

[3] Arabic: *shirk.*
[4] Arabic: *waseela.*
[5] Arabic: w*asita.*
[6] Arabic: permitted – *halal;* forbidden – *haram.*

that says meditation is forbidden. It is only for God to make something permissible or forbidden.

The Prophet ﷺ said, "What is forbidden is clear and what is permitted is clear."

Those who declare the practice of making meditation to the Sufi guide forbidden have no authority to do so. They are stating their opinions, and their opinions do not carry the weight of scholarship or law.

They are foolish people, indeed, who believe that one can reach the Divine Presence without a vehicle, without relying on a means. It is as though they are saying, "We may reach the moon without using anything. We may jump from here to there!" What is the purpose of knowledge if one does not use it?

Such people tell those who listen to them that all the knowledge they need, can be found in the Holy Qur'an. They say, "Read the Qur'an and you will understand." That is destroying Islam. It is God's Ancient Holy Words.[7] How then, can they say that everyone can recite and understand such a sublime text? On the contrary, God said:

> If they had only referred it to the Messenger, and to
> those in authority among them, those among them who
> can search out the knowledge of it would have known it.
> (4:83)

You must listen to those servants who have been granted authority. Only they can discern the real meanings from what is necessary to be known. Only they may comb the oceans of Divine Knowledge and bring back pearls. Not everyone may comb through the oceans and bring back pearls. That means, if you are unsure about something, you must find such a person—one who is bringing pearls of meaning.

---

[7] Arabic: *kalamullah al-qadeem.*

God has given that understanding only to those special people whom He has authorized to receive it. Not everyone understands. Those who believe otherwise are falling into unbelief (*kufr*). So, too, are those who—acting upon this misguided belief that the full knowledge of the Holy Qur'an is available to all—declare that the practice of making meditation to a Sufi guide is unbelief fall into unbelief themselves. The irony of their claim is that, through meditation with the Sufi guide, one may come to a real understanding of the Qur'an.

May God forgive me and bless you. *Al-Fatiha*.

Shaykh Muhammad Nazim Adil al-Haqqani
Lefke, Cyprus
Ramadan 17, 1425/October 30, 2004

Introduction

by Shaykh Muhammad Hisham Kabbani

THE KNOWLEDGE OF THE SAINTS

*G*od ordered us:

> *Obey God, obey the Prophet and obey those*
> *who are in authority. (4:59)*

God's Knowledge never ends. Human knowledge ends. So it follows that any knowledge[1] taken from God's Knowledge never ends, while any knowledge that is taken from people or from the world of illusion[2] ends. That is why those who take knowledge from schools, universities, seminars and lectures will find that, at some point, their knowledge is going to end. However, knowledge that is taken from the heart of the Prophet Muhammad ﷺ remains constant, for the Prophet ﷺ is taking from the reality of one of God's Divine Attribute's, The All-Knowing[3]. The Prophet ﷺ is in full manifestation of that name. He was taking from that Ocean of Knowledge in the time of the Companions[4] and after their time, and the Prophet ﷺ is still giving that knowledge to the hearts of the saints.[5] That is real knowledge. It increases, but it does not change. It accumulates, building upon itself, adding more and more – from level one, to level two, to level three..... accumulating infinitely.

---

[1] Arabic: *'ilm.*

[2] Arabic: *dunya.*

[3] Arabic: *Al-'Aleem*

[4] Arabic: *sahaba*: Companions of the Prophet

[5] Arabic: *awliya*: saints (sing. *wali*)

God is All-Knowing and He is the only Creator. Thus, while God's own knowledge is without end, just as He is constantly creating, He is constantly opening new knowledge to His Creation. God is constantly adding to the Oceans of Knowledge that are accessible to His creation, and the Prophet ﷺ is constantly taking knowledge from that Ocean and giving it to the saints and, through them, to his Community of Believers[6].

God said:

> *Behold! Verily on the friends of God there is no fear,*
> *nor shall they grieve.* (10:62)

Note that God refers to saints in the plural. God said, "Verily my saints, they have nothing to fear and nothing to be afraid of and they will never be sad." It means nothing can frighten them. The rejection of people does not frighten them for even Prophet Muhammad's ﷺ own tribe rejected him. Saints care not whether people reject or accept them, for they are inheritors of the Prophet ﷺ and thus inheritors of the Truth the Prophet ﷺ is carrying.

However, in this verse, God is not just saying that His saints have nothing to be afraid of. He is also telling them not to despair of His Mercy. He is telling them that His Mercy will continue to come to them through *Sayyidina* Muhammad ﷺ, both in this world and in the next. God is telling the saints that they must not lose heart if people reject them. God is telling them that He is putting them at the head of the Community by putting them in the society of His Messenger. God is elevating His saints to higher and higher levels of authority by allowing them to abide in the presence of *Sayyidina* Muhammad ﷺ. As his station ascends, so too does theirs. Wherever he is going, he is taking them with him. They cannot be left behind, for they are the true lovers of *Sayyidina* Muhammad ﷺ; the true lovers of God.

---

[6] *ummah:* The Community of Believers

The saints are like cars in a great train, pulled ever forward by the Prophet Muhammad ﷺ. The Prophet ﷺ is like the locomotive. Each of the saints is hooked to that engine and follows it wherever it goes. Wherever the Prophet ﷺ goes, the saints will follow. The saints carry with them all of the believers in the same manner as passengers are carried in train cars. Saints are like the vehicles connected to the Prophet ﷺ, and God has honored them to fill their carriages with their followers. Saints are taking their followers to the Prophet ﷺ.

On the Night of the Journey and the Ascension[7] when the Prophet ﷺ was called to God, he did not leave his community behind, nor did he leave behind his inheritors. *Sayyidina* Muhammad ﷺ took them in his heart, for he is the Mercy to All Creation.[8] He brought them with him through the power that God granted him, for God states in His Holy Qur'an:

Let it be known that the Prophet of God is in you.
(49:7)[9]

His power is in us – and if *Sayyidina* Muhammad ﷺ is in us, that means that God is giving him that authority. That is not attributing partners to God[10]. God revealed this verse so that we might know that the Prophet's power is in us, that the Prophet's gaze is focused upon us, that he is meditating upon us, and that he is making meditation[11] to bring his Community with him to God's Presence to be cleaned and purified.

---

[7] Arabic: *Laylat al-Isra wal-Mi'raj*: Night Journey and Ascension

[8] Arabic: *rahmatan lil-'alameen*: Mercy to All Creation

[9] Arabic: *wa 'alamu anna feekum rasulullah.*

[10] Arabic: *shirk*: Attributing partners to God

[11] Arabic: *muraqabah*: meditation.

On the Night of the Journey and the Ascension, when the Prophet ﷺ was in the Divine Presence, God showed him his Community. They were all there. He honored them to be in the Divine Presence. God said, "O Muhammad, this is your Community." Each one was pure and clean, just as they were born. The Prophet ﷺ said, "Human beings are born in purity and innocence."

This was how they appeared to the Prophet ﷺ, and God asked him, "Do you accept them as a trust?" The Prophet ﷺ said, "Yes, I will take them." He took them and he said, "O my Lord, I will take that trust and I will carry them."[12]

Sayyidina Muhammad ﷺ was happy, for he was seeing his Community in the pure state in which God created them. That is why saints are happy with their followers, because they see them under God's Mercy[13]. God's Mercy burns away the sins of people. It cleanses them. Thus, when the Prophet ﷺ saw his Community so clean and so pure, he said, "Yes, I accept," and he took them in.

As soon as the Prophet ﷺ said, "I am accepting," God showed him their realities, that they were going to follow Satan and the countless sins they were going to commit. God showed him that only a few of them would be protected—the Friends of God.[14] God put them under His Protection.

When the Prophet ﷺ saw all their sins, he was worried. He said, "O my Lord, give me helpers." Of course, the Prophet ﷺ did not need helpers, but he was showing humbleness before his Lord. God said, "I will give you what you ask," and He gave him helpers equal to the

---

[12] God said: *My mercy extendeth to all things. That (mercy) I shall ordain for those who do right...* (7:156) All Muslims say *la ilaha ill-God Muhammadu rasulullah.* That is the first step into belief. No one can say that anyone who says this is not a Muslim. Grandshaykh Abdullah ad-Daghestani also teaches us that in the world of souls (*'alam al-arwaah*), on the Day of Promises, before we came to earth, everyone was saying, "O God, you are our Lord." They were all believers. He said, "That means that God will give to Sayyidina Muhammad whoever he likes." No one can say "no" to God.

[13] Arabic: *Rahmat*

[14] Arabic: *awliyaullah:* Friends of God (sing. *waliullah*)

number of his Companions. He gave him 124,000 saints and He divided the Community between them.

Some of the saints were given 100 million people to look after. Some were given 200 million. Some were given one billion. Each saint took his share. Even though the saint might not meet each of his charges physically, they are always looking after them. These Sufi guides may reach them in dreams, or through other spiritual means. They might be scattered all around the world in different countries, but their Sufi guide will always reach them, one way or another. They may not even know that they are with that master, but he knows that they are with him and he hooks each one to his wagon. Each night, in the Prayer of Salvation[15], the master presents them to the Prophet ﷺ, taking responsibility for them in the presence of the Prophet ﷺ and asking forgiveness[16] on their behalf. When he does, the Prophet ﷺ asks forgiveness on behalf of that saint and his followers from God, and God bestows His Mercy and Forgiveness on them.

The Sufi guide is like the driver of a horse-drawn carriage. The driver sits outside the carriage, on a high seat so that he can see what lies ahead. The passengers ride inside the carriage. They cannot see the road ahead—only whether it is day or evening. They go where the driver takes them. The saints are like these drivers, each one following the Prophet ﷺ in a long train of carriages. Sitting atop their carriages, they can see the Prophet ﷺ. They can see whatever signals come from that lead wagon. The passengers riding inside their carriages cannot. However, the driver—the Sufi guide—can relate to them whatever he sees coming from the Prophet ﷺ.

The saints are the only ones who have this direct vision of the Prophet ﷺ[17] and the ability to communicate what they see to their passengers. Yet the clarity of their vision is not equal. Each carriage forms part of a

---

[15] Arabic: *Salaat an-Najaat*: a special prayer consisting of two cycles, observed in the early watches of the night before the dawn prayer (Fajr). In it the shaykh prays for forgiveness and salvation for all his followers, individual by individual.

[16] Arabic: *istighfaar*: forgiveness

[17] Arabic: *kashf*: direct vision of the Prophet ﷺ

train behind the Prophet ﷺ. Some are near the front of that train, others near the end. The saint sitting atop the first carriage can see the Prophet ﷺ more clearly than the saint who is riding atop the tenth carriage, or the hundredth carriage, or the 124,000th carriage at the end of the train. The one at the end cannot see anything except shadows, some faint images very far away. Still, he is seeing, and he is relating what he sees to his followers. The perspective of every driver depends on his proximity to the front of the carriage train, on his proximity to the Prophet ﷺ. The closer a saint is to the Prophet ﷺ, the more knowledge he receives and the more he can relate to his followers.

Each saint is making Sufi meditation. Each one is meditating on the Prophet ﷺ at the head of the train of carriages. Each one is focusing on the Prophet ﷺ and the Prophet ﷺ is focusing to the Divine Presence. This is the chain by which each is connected. The saint is focusing on the Prophet ﷺ and looking at his followers. He is interacting with the Prophet ﷺ by focusing on the Prophet ﷺ; but within him are his followers, because God gave him that carriage and He gave him that authority. The followers inside the carriage are focusing on their driver, looking at how he is driving. They are focusing on the saint who is running the horses, who is steering the carriage. Therefore, everyone is in the presence of everyone else. They are present in each other.

Moreover, the Sufi guide is intervening with and for his followers. In this way, they are interlocking—one with another. They are woven together like a carpet. All the threads are woven together; they are connected to each other. If you pull one thread, the carpet begins to fall apart. They have to be together. The Sufi guide cannot leave his followers, nor can he take his focus from them.

Similarly, the disciple[18] must maintain his connection with the guide. He cannot allow himself to become disconnected. He must leave himself and be connected to the Master's presence. The Shaykh carries his followers to the Presence of the Prophet ﷺ, so they must be in his presence completely. The Prophet ﷺ will carry the carriage

---

[18] Arabic: *mureed:* A disciple or follower of a Sufi guide.

with that Shaykh in his heart, just as he carries all 124,000 saints and their carriages. In the end, all of them will be carried to the presence of *Sayyidina* Muhammad 🙵 and he will carry them to the Presence of God. The final goal of Sufi meditation is to reach the Divine Presence, but it is a journey that must first pass through these intermediary stages.

SUFI MEDITATION: THE HEART CONNECTION

Associations are an important part of this Way. Every association needs a connection to the main source in order for the speaker to give the listeners what is needed. Anyone can talk, but what they say may not benefit those that they are talking to. Every listener has something in his heart and in his mind. The speaker needs to satisfy those needs. When they plug in to that main source, they know what everyone needs to hear.

When our master, Mawlana Shaykh Nazim, begins an association, he says, "*Madad ya Sayyidi. Dastoor ya sayyidi. madad al-haqq, Mawlana Grandshaykh Abdullah.*"[19] In doing so, he is requesting that connection. To make that connection, he is focusing and concentrating on his Shaykh, Mawlana Grandshaykh Abdullah, directly, and he is asking that Grandshaykh inspire his heart with that which he has inherited from the heart of the Prophet 🙵. He is seeking a connection from his heart, to Grandshaykh's heart, to the heart of the Prophet 🙵. This is the state of Sufi meditation, and Mawlana Shaykh Nazim is always in it, always connected to the heart of his Grandshaykh and, through him, to the heart of the Prophet 🙵. In this way, he is able to take whatever is necessary for his audience.

---

[19] "*Madad ya Sayyidi. Dastoor ya sayyidi, madad al-haqq:* I ask support from you, my master. I ask permission from you, my master. I ask your support, O Truthful one.

Grandshaykh knows what information to send because he is looking to the heart of Shaykh Nazim, and Shaykh Nazim's heart is like a telescope, moving around the hearts of his followers, panning through the crowd like a camera. Based on what he sees in their hearts, different kinds of information will be sent. It might be general information if it is a public talk, or it might be knowledge and information meant for certain people that only they can understand. Whatever comes, the means of transmission is the same—one looking and focusing on the other.

When your Sufi master says *Madad*, it means that he is making that heart connection[20] to the heart of his Shaykh. It means he is in a state of meditation (*muraqabah*) to the heart of his Shaykh, and his Shaykh is in a state of meditation to the heart of the Prophet ﷺ, and the Prophet ﷺ is in a state of meditation in the Divine Presence.

Sufi meditation may take place both in person or at a distance. When the disciple makes meditation on the Shaykh in his presence, he is in constant focus on the Shaykh, observing everything – how he acts, how he eats, how he drinks—in order that he might imitate him one day. Sufi meditation means looking in order to learn.

We must always be looking at the Shaykh, focusing on what he is doing. This is how we learn—what we have to say, what we have to read, what we have to do. We learn by observing the master. That is the discipline of this Order, to observe and to follow. We do this by focusing on the Shaykh through Sufi meditation.

You can also do meditation from a distance, because the master is always present with his followers. One time my brother and I wanted to go to visit Grandshaykh and Mawlana Shaykh Nazim. We were in Beirut and they were in Damascus. Our mother was not allowing us to go, because we were students at the university and we had homework to do, but we insisted on going. We were feeling the presence of the

---

[20] *Muraqiban*: connection

Shaykh. We were feeling him with us. With our great love for him, it was as if we were in his presence.

It is like when a boy is in love with a girl. Before marriage, he is always thinking about her, thinking about when he can speak with her, when he can see her, when he can go out with her. Because of that love, he is taken to a higher level—the level of presence. The boy wants to be in her presence and the girl wants to be his presence.

Of course, the pure, unconditional love for the Shaykh is even stronger. It will certainly take you to be in his presence. It will make you want to give up everything for his sake, to give up the material world of illusions [21] for the sake of the spiritual world of realities.[22] The hereafter

is better than this worldly life, and the Shaykh represents the hereafter, because he guides you to the hereafter. Thus, you want to be in his presence. That feeling of presence is the real Sufi meditation. It is called the presence of the Shaykh (*hudoor ash-shaykh*[23]). Wherever you go, you see the master. Through that love, it is as if you are looking at your spiritual teacher and he is looking at you.

That was how we felt, and that was why we wanted to go. Our mother said, "No. Do not go." We said, "We are going." We were young, so we quarreled, fought and left. When we arrived after many hours of driving, we came to the door but just before we knocked, Grandshaykh opened the door. How did he know we were there? Because he was observing us, surveying us from a distance and watching us. That is meditation of the Sufi master to his followers. He said, "Go back. Do not come to me after fighting with your mother. Go back and fix your

---

[21]Arabic: *dunya:* The material world of illusions; the world we live in.

[22]Arabic: *akhira:* The spiritual world of realities; the Hereafter.

[23] *hudoor ash-shaykh:* the presence of the Shaykh

problem with your mother, then come back to me." He did not let us into his house. We had no choice but to go back.

We can see another example in the story of *Sayyidina* Umar ఉ and Sariya ఉ. *Sayyidina* Umar ఉ was not a prophet, he was a Companion. However, *Sayyidina* Umar ఉ, using meditation, was able to control his army in Syria while standing on the pulpit delivering the Friday sermon in Madinah—a distance of over 1500 miles. During the sermon he suddenly broke off and began calling out in a loud voice to his commander Sariya ఉ, "O Sariya, look at the mountain." Sariya, who was also using meditation, heard him and was able to save his army from the enemy. This is not ascribing partners to God nor is it unbelief.[24] Meditation is a vehicle that the Sufi master allows you to use in order to reach him, just as it was allowed *Sayyidina* Umar ఉ to reach Sariya ఉ.

If you have a single wire, you cannot build an electric circuit. Every electric circuit must have two wires in order for energy to flow through it. A spiritual circuit works in the same way. There must be one wire from you and one wire from the Guide. God gave each of us a wire in our heart. The Guide's wire is always positive. Your wire is negative. The Guide takes your negativity and fills you up with positive energy. The Guide says to you, "Although you are a bad person, doing this wrong and that mistake, still I am going to give you positive energy."

Of course, a circuit does not work unless it is plugged in. The plug is the vehicle through which the electricity travels from the power source to the circuit. If the circuit is not plugged in, nothing will happen. The Guide is like that plug. He connects you to the Source of Divine Power. The purpose of the Guide in your life is to connect these two wires to the plug. When you are connected—to the Guide and through the Guide—then true visions may come to you. The Guide can see you, because he is the Guide. From your side, you need to focus on him so that he can connect the two wires. Then the circuit is completed and the power flows. Thus in the example of Sariya ఉ, he had one wire and

---

[24]Arabic: *kufr*: unbelief

Sayyidina Umar ﷺ had the other, and they were able to plug them in and work together.

There are some today who question the importance of Sufi meditation. Others say that it is unbelief or *shirk*. In fact, it is one of the most important spiritual disciplines of Islam. Even Ibn Taymiyya, the teacher of the Wahhabi school, discussed Sufi meditation in his *Compendium*.[25] He related the story of two very sincere, pious brothers who were so much in love with each other that God—through that love—gave them the power to help each other in everything. If one of the brothers was sick, so was the other. If one found himself in difficulty, the other suffered with him.

One day, the two brothers were performing ablution by a river. As one was washing himself, he fell into the water. The water was deep and the river was running fast. It took him, and he did not know how to swim. The other brother did not know how to swim either, but—because of his attachment to his brother—he could not stand to be separated from him, even though he was drowning in the river. Therefore, he jumped into the water. He wanted to be with his brother. His brother said, "What did you do?" He replied, "I cannot leave you." That connection—that need—to be in his brother's presence, attracted him.

Ibn Taymiyya related this story to explain Sufi meditation, to explain the Station of Presence and the Station of Annihilation. He said, "This is the real state of annihilation. At that time there is no I and me, there is only one." He described these states as love, as presence and as annihilation.

---

[25] *Majmu'a fatawa ibn taymiyya.*

THE THREE STATIONS

There are three stations in this Order[26], and each of these stations has three levels.

The first station is the Station of Love: the love of God[27], the love of the Prophet ﷺ[28] and the love of the Guide.[29] If love of the Guide were not important, it would not be listed among these. However, in the Sufi path[30], you must first acquire the love of the Shaykh, then he guides you to the love of the Prophet ﷺ and the Prophet ﷺ guides you to the love of God.

The second is the Station of Presence. The first level of this station is the presence of the Shaykh. You have to be in that presence always. You have to be in continuous meditation to the Shaykh. The presence of the Shaykh will take you to Presence of the Prophet ﷺ and the Prophet ﷺ will take you to the Presence of God. That takes you to the final station, the Station of Annihilation.

The first step towards the Station of Annihilation is annihilation in the Guide[31]. Here, the self is finished. There is no more will. Everything is submitted to the will of the Guide. This takes you to annihilation in Prophet ﷺ, and that takes you to annihilation in the Presence of God.[32]

Grandshaykh said, "After reaching the level of love of the Shaykh, after reaching the level of presence of the Shaykh, you reach the level of annihilation in the Shaykh. Real annihilation is such that, if one gets a wound and is bleeding, the other one must get a wound in the same place and bleed."

---

[26] *tariqat*: Sufi order

[27] *mahabat-Allah*: the love of God

[28] *mahabat al-Habib*: the love of the Prophet

[29] *mahabat ash-Shaykh*: the love of the Shaykh

[30] *Tariqah*: the Sufi path; a specific lineage named for its founder.

[31] *fana fi'sh-shaykh*: annihilation in the Shaykh

[32] *fana fillah*: annihilation in the Presence of God

When one reaches the level of annihilation in the Shaykh, he experiences what the Shaykh experiences. When the Shaykh is happy, he is happy. If the Shaykh gets a burden, he gets a burden. They feel with each other. Their feelings are focused to one feeling, so that each of them feels the same. That is called the Station of the Gardens.[33]

When God resurrects you and sends you to Paradise, everyone will be the same—just like on the Plain of Arafat. Everyone will be focused on their Lord. When you are there, you will make meditation to the Divine Presence, because you will be in that Presence. If your Guide is there, you cannot speak. It is similar to the time during Hajj when you are at Arafat. There, your guide[34] is the one who makes the supplication[35] on behalf of the entire group. Everyone else just says, *Ameen.*

On this Way, you must have a guide, someone whom you look to for guidance and whom you follow on the Path. He is the one who guides you to the Prophet ﷺ. He is the one who guides you to God. When he guides you to God, then you can be a guide. Then you will be a Guide. Until then, you need a Shaykh to guide you.

When you make the Pilgrimage to Makkah[36], you see that most people are walking. Many of them are in groups, and each of these groups has a leader. How do they keep track of their leader in this vast sea of humanity? Each one carries something—a flag, a banner, a turban on a stick—so that those who are traveling with him can see where he is going and follow him. If you are part of one of those groups, you are focusing on that symbol, focusing on that flag, on that banner, on whatever device your guide is holding. If you are far away, you cannot see your guide, but you can see his symbol. You follow that symbol, and it leads you to the place where you stone the pillars which represent the devil. There you find your guide, and he tells you to throw your stones

---

[33] *maqam al-jinan*: Stations of the Gardens.

[34] *mutawif*: guide.

[35] *Du'a*: supplication or prayer.

[36] *Hajj*: Pilgrimmage to Makkah

at Satan and say, "God is greatest. I am opposing Satan, seeking the pleasure of the Most Merciful."[37]

Sufi meditation is like that. When you are separated from your Guide, you must focus on his symbol so that you can continue to receive guidance from him. You concentrate on his image in your heart. Even though you are far away, you see him and you come to him and he takes you to that place where you can cast Satan out of your heart and reach God's Mercy.

THE SUFI BOND: FORGING THE CHAIN

When you make the Pilgrimage and you are assigned to a group, that is your bond (*rabitah*). When you join a group and place yourself under its leader, that is your bond (*rabitah*). It is a communal action that is undertaken with the other members of that group. Sufi meditation, on the other hand, is a private act that one does alone.

Each Sufi teacher oversees a group. That master is connected to each of his followers and, together, they form his chain. However, within that group, each of his students is on his own. Each one is individually responsible for his or her relationship with the teacher. Yet the Sufi

teacher sees each one as part of his group. This is the essence of the Sufi bond, *rabitah*. When you are initiated into the Order, you are establishing that link. You are forging your bond with the Guide. Then, when someone asks you which group you are with, you say,

---

[37] "*Allahu Akbar, raghman li 'sh-shaytan ridan li 'l-rahman*"

"I am with Shaykh Nazim. I am connected to him. I am with him." Initiation is a promise and, when we make that promise, we are included in that Order—in that *rabitah*.

Through the Sufi Bond you are connected to your group. It is like when the pilgrimage guide is taking you to stone Satan, he is taking the entire group. Some people are at the end and some people are near the guide. Those who are directly behind the guide can see him always. They can even hold onto his cloak. However, the ones at the end, they can only see the guide's symbol, the flag. So it is with the Guide. There are some advanced students who are always behind the Guide, always in his presence, always seeing him. They are in the Station of Presence. Then there are those who are at the end of the group, who cannot see the Guide, but can only see his symbol—his flag or his turban. They are not in his presence. They are still in the Station of Love, but not in the Station of Presence. Nevertheless, all are in his chain, they are in his *rabitah*, they are connected and they cannot be excluded.

All of those sitting in the Guide's presence have already accepted his hand and been initiated into the Order, so the association is the *rabitah*, affirming their connection to each other. All of them are connected to the same guide. This is the meaning of the Sufi bond. It connects all of those who are spread out in different places and brings them together. Though the Sufi teacher and his followers are scattered all over the world, he connects them through the Sufi bond linking them to his chain.

In the Middle East, we use the term *rabitah* in reference to our families. It signifies that we share a common relationship. As there is a physical bond through blood relations, so there is a spiritual bond through spiritual relations. Blood relatives have a bond between them that connects them all. Those who are connected in spiritual bond (*rabitah*) are those who are under the same Sufi teacher. He connects their souls, which were put under his care on the Day of Promises and on the Night of the Journey and the Ascension by the Prophet ﷺ. That connection is under his control, under his power. That is his *rabitah*.

That is why, in *Khatmu 'l-Khwajagan*[38], when we perform the *dhikr*[39], we say, *Rabitatu 'sh-Sharifah*. It means connect your heart to that bond and to remember that you are tied to that rope, that you are part of the chain of the Sufi teacher. When the Shaykh says, *rabitah*, it means you must renew your initiation in your heart. You must affirm your pledge of allegiance to him, as if you were saying, "O my Master, I am still in your chain. Please, do not take me out. I am still there." When we say *rabitah*, we are reaffirming our connection with our Guide, renewing our relationship with him and remembering that he connects us with the Prophet ﷺ and, through the Prophet ﷺ, connects us with the Divine Presence.

Keep that relationship of spiritual childhood with the teacher and that relationship of brotherhood with his other followers. The teacher is like the father, and the other followers are like your brothers and sisters. That is your connection. Know to whom you are related. We are related to al-Haqqani, who is related to ad-Daghestani – to Mawlana Shaykh 'Abdullah ق and Shaykh Sharafuddin Daghestani ق – related to Abu Muhammad al-Madani ق related to Sayyid Jamaluddin al-Ghumuqi al-Husseini ق [40], all the way back to the Prophet ﷺ. This is our connection. This is our Sufi bond, our *rabitah*. This is the chain by which we reach there.

THE DISTINCTION BETWEEN SUFI MEDITATION AND THE SUFI BOND

To understand the distinction between Sufi meditation (*muraqabah*) and the Sufi bond (*rabitah*), consider a hotel. Inside the hotel, there may be a thousand rooms. Each room has a key. The keys are kept on a chain. The doorkeeper keeps all the keys to all the rooms on a big chain, so each one is connected to the other one and none of them can be lost.

---

[38] *Khatmu 'l-Khwajagan:* Circle of the Masters, a specific liturgical form of remembering God according to the Masters of Wisdom of the Naqshbandi Sufi Order.

[39] *dhikr:* literally, the remembrance of God; Sufi orders often have specific recitations of Qur'an and Divine Attributes. Dhikr can be done silently or aloud; singly or in a group. It is recited for connecting and healing of the heart.

That chain represents *rabitah*. They are all connected and, everywhere the master of that hotel he goes, he takes the chain with him.

Each key on that chain is unique. Each one opens an individual door, and is the only key that can unlock the door to that particular room. The guests in that hotel are students of the Teacher, and each one is given a key to unlock their own room. When they use that key, unlock the door and enter that room that represents Sufi meditation (*muraqabah*).

In addition to the guests, the hotel also has a staff. There are cleaning people, and each one of them is given the key to a number of rooms that it is their responsibility to care for. They have a master key that unlocks five rooms, ten rooms or twenty rooms. It depends on how much authority the manager of the hotel gave them. These are the representatives of the Teacher, and their job is to clean up the dirt of the guests. That means their job is to prepare the followers.

The manager of the hotel has a master key that unlocks all of the doors. He is the Guide, and he can open all the doors of the hearts of his followers. He is in direct connection with them.

SUFI MEDITATION: THE MEANS AND THE END

Grandshaykh related the following story:

One time, Shaykh Abdul Qadir Jilani ق said to his followers, those under his Sufi bond, "Today, I want every one of you to go and slaughter a chicken in a place where no one can see you." They went, everyone hiding themselves—behind the mountains, behind the hills, behind the market, behind houses, behind bushes, behind trees, on the water and wherever else they were able to in Baghdad. They tried their best to do it. After an hour, one of the shaykh's followers returned with a dead rooster. Another one came back after two hours. One came after three hours. One at a time, they returned until only one was left. He did not return. The time for the evening prayer came, and still they could not find him.

The next day, he returned carrying a live rooster in his hands, coming to Shaykh Abdul Qadir Jilani. The shaykh said, "All of your friends came, and they have slaughtered their roosters already. Why were you late? I asked you to hide yourself in a place where no one could see you, slaughter the chicken and come back to me. What happened to you?" He said, "O my master, you asked me to slaughter the chicken where no one could see me. I was looking and thinking, focusing and meditating. I went to the hill to slaughter the rooster where no one could see me, but I saw you there. I went to the beach where no one could see me, but I saw you there. I went to the forest, and with my meditation, I saw you there. Wherever I went, you were present. I could not find an empty space where you were not there with me, where I was not in your presence. Through your presence I found myself in the presence of the Prophet ﷺ, reaching even to the presence of God. Therefore, I realized there was no place empty in this world – in this universe – that was empty of you, empty of the Prophet ﷺ, empty of God. Wherever I directed my face, I was seeing you. Wherever I directed my face, I was feeling the presence of the Prophet ﷺ. Wherever I directed my face, I was feeling the Presence of God. So how could I slaughter the rooster? I was in continuous meditation, and you were everywhere." After hearing his disciple's answer, Shaykh Abdul Qadir Jilani said, "You are my representative."[41] You are the only one that understood the meaning of meditation and *rabitah*, may God support you. I am sending you as an authorized person, to spread my teachings around the world."

Grandshaykh also related another story about Shaykh Abdul Qadir Jilani ق:

One time, one of the shaykh's followers died. *Sayyidina* Azraeel, the Angel of Death came, took his soul and went. They buried him. Then Ankar and Nakir came—the two angels who come to question a person after death. They are not easy. They are strong with the power that God gave them. They began to question the man, but to every question, he

---

[40] These are some of the names of Shaykhs in the Naqshbandi tariqat which form an unbroken chain of spiritual transmission from Shaykh Nazim al-Haqqani all the way back to the Prophet Muhammad ﷺ

[41] Arabic: *Khalifa*.

just answered, "Abdul Qadir Jilani." They asked, "Who is your Creator?" He said, "Abdul Qadir Jilani." "What is your religion?" "Abdul Qadir Jilani." "What is your Holy Book?" "Abdul Qadir Jilani." To every question, he replied, "Abdul Qadir Jilani." It was his way of saying, "I am annihilated in Abdul Qadir Jilani. Do not ask me—ask him. I was always, in the material world, in his presence. In the hereafter, I am in his presence." Therefore, the shaykh was obliged to answer Ankar and Nakir on his behalf. Instantly he appeared there before them to do just that. Shaykh Abdul Qadir Jilani said, "If you grind him, if you grind his body and his blood and reduce it to tiny pieces, every one of his cells and every drop of his blood is going to say, Abdul Qadir Jilani.'"

This disciple had reached the level of Presence with the Shaykh. The first station is Love: Love of the Shaykh, Love of Prophet ﷺ, Love of God. The Station of Presence is the station of Sufi meditation. That disciple was still in the first level of the Station of Presence. Sufi meditation filled him completely, but he had not yet been able to go to the second level, which is meditation on the Prophet ﷺ.[42] He was in transition when he died. If he had been able to reach the next level, it would have led him to meditation on God,[43] which is the ultimate goal: meditation with the Divine Presence. He reached it later, in the grave.

The beginning has to be through the spiritual master. The shaykh will take you to the Prophet ﷺ. This is the discipline of the Sufi orders, obedience, for God says:

Obey God, obey Prophet, and obey those in authority over you. (4:59)

Thus, meditation has to be with the shaykh, in the shaykh and looking at the shaykh.

Consider a driver's education car. In it, you have the instructor and a student driver. The instructor has a steering wheel, gas pedal

[42]Arabic: *Muraqabatu 'r-Rasul*: meditation on the Prophet ﷺ.

[43] Arabic: *Muraqabatullah*: meditation on God.

and brake. The student has the same thing. The student drives and the teacher observes and directs him. If the student makes a mistake, his teacher corrects him. Thus, the student is in continuous meditation with his instructor while he is driving. It is the same in the Sufi orders. The student is in continuous meditation with his spiritual guide. If he makes a mistake, the Guide pulls him up quickly.

Rabitah has to be to the Guide. Sufi meditation has to be to the Guide. *Rabitah* is always to the Guide because you are in his chain, and he takes you and ties you to the rope of the Prophet ﷺ and the Prophet ﷺ ties you to the rope of God. For, as God says in the Holy Qur'an:

> *Hold tight to the rope of God, and do not separate.*
> *(3:103)*

Rabitah is to attach yourself to the Guide, to the Prophet ﷺ and to God by taking initiation or renewing it. Sufi meditation is a method you must follow throughout your lifetime in order to discipline yourself and learn the characteristics and good behavior of the Guide. The Companions used to look at the Prophet ﷺ and try to follow in his footsteps, and God said:

> *If you really love God follow me, God will love you.*
> *(3:31)*

Sufi meditation is to follow the footsteps of the Prophet ﷺ, which also means following the footsteps of the inheritors of the Prophet ﷺ. It takes you first to love—the love of the Guide, the love of the Prophet ﷺ and to the love of God. Then it takes you to a higher station, to the Presence of the Guide, the Presence of the Prophet ﷺ and to the Presence of God. Then it takes you to Annihilation in the Guide, Annihilation in Prophet ﷺ and Annihilation in God.

Those are the three stations. They are parallel to the three stations of certainty: Knowledge of Certainty[44], the Vision of Certainty[45], and the Reality of Certainty[46].

Love gives you Knowledge; Presence gives you Vision and Annihilation gives you Reality. With love, you can hear and the Knowledge of Certainty comes to you by hearing. Presence means you are in the presence of the Guide, making meditation, focusing on him. That is why it leads you to the reality of seeing. Annihilation is paralleled by the Reality of Certainty, for it is the real truth. This is the way of Sufi meditation. This is guidance for you on your spiritual journey.

May God send us His Mercy and His Forgiveness.

Shaykh Muhammad Hisham Kabbani
Fenton, Michigan
Dhul-Hijjah 1, 1425/January 12, 2005

---

[44] Arabic: *'Ilmu 'l-yaqeen*: Knowledge of Certainty.

[45] Arabic: *'Aynu 'l-Yaqeen*: Vision of Certainty.

[46] Arabic: *Haqqu 'l-Yaqeen*: Reality of Certainty.

Chapter
1

Sufi Meditation
(Muraqabah)

Sufi Meditation

(Muraqabah)

SECTION ONE: SUFI MEDITATION DEFINED

*C*onsistent and daily Sufi meditation (muraqabah) is essential to the progress of the follower of a shaykh towards the rending of veils and victory over this illusionary world.

Sufi meditation is synonymous with the technical Sufi term which translates to "Noble Connection" and has always been a central practice of Islamic spirituality—Sufism. This science of contemplation is the subject of an entire section in the works of Imam Ghazzali ق, and it has always been a core practice of the Masters of the Naqshbandi Order. Sufi meditation may also be seen as synonymous with the more general practice of meditation that is so central to many of the Eastern spiritual traditions, the goal of which has always been the fusion of the individual back into the oneness of the Universal Reality.

The default condition of mankind is immersion in the illusion of this world. For the uninitiated, that illusion is reality—the material world of the senses is all that exists. However, as we progress along the path of spiritual development, our understanding of reality changes. We learn that this world is completely unreal. We come to understand that there is another reality—an authentic reality—behind this realm of illusion, a reality from which we are veiled, but which, nonetheless, is the only reality that really matters to us.

Once we reach this level of understanding, once we come to accept the illusory nature of the world around us and begin to discern the reality that lies behind it, we begin searching for a doorway through which we can pass out of this realm of delusion into the realm of realities. Sufi meditation is that doorway.

Through Sufi meditation, we detach ourselves from this false world and immerse ourselves in reality. Only by cutting ourselves off from the unending onslaught of the senses, by tuning out the distractions of this world, can we hope to escape from its tyranny and oppression.

We must recognize that there is no special reward for doing what is required. If we perform the daily prayers, pay the poor-tax, fast during Ramadan, and make the hajj, we will only have done what our Lord commanded—thereby, God-willing ensuring our salvation in the next life. But there is no trophy for completing these basic requirements. There is no trophy for fleeing from a burning building—the one who escapes the fire by virtue of that fact alone. If we want greater rewards than that we must look farther. Those who want to reach higher stations must work harder.

Endless treasures await those who strive towards their Lord, but each treasure has its key that must be unearthed. Performing supererogatory devotions, praying extra prayers, and making remembrance of God and recitation of His Names and recitations of prayers (all such remembrance and recitation is referred to under the general Sufi term of "remembrance" or *dhikr*) are all keys that unlock such secrets. But the most important key, the one that unlocks the door to the Divine Presence, is Sufi meditation.

All prophets came to their peoples urging them to see beyond this world to the heavenly plane beyond this life. But we cannot enter into this new world without leaving the old one behind. First, we must extricate ourselves from the tangled web of ego and attachments that binds us here. This act of extrication is referred to as "negation." When we manage to negate ourselves, when we manage to die before we die, then we enter fully into the world of realities.

Sufi meditation is the first step on this path of self-negation. The practice of Sufi meditation has no rational explanation in the terms of this world, because in its essence it is a negation of this world. It is based on spiritual rather than material principles—chief among being the existence of two types of sight which function simultaneously in each person.

PRINCIPLES OF SIGHT

One form of sight is limited and requires a medium in which to function. The other is unlimited, functioning independently of any medium.

The medium within which the first form of sight functions is physical space. This form of seeing can only perceive that which exists in the dimensions of physical space. Even within those dimensions, it is extremely limited. For example, it can only detect that which reflects or emits wavelengths of light within a narrow band of the electromagnetic spectrum. It cannot perceive very small objects without the aid of special mechanical or electronic aids. It can only encompass objects with an unobstructed line to the person who sees. This mode of seeing also relies on physical action of the eyes to transmit the images they perceive onto the screen of the mind.

The other form of seeing is free of such limitations, and functions on the plane of heavenly realities. The images it apprehends are projected directly onto the screen of the mind without the intervention of external organs. It is this mode of sight that functions during Sufi meditation.

THE PATH OF SUFI MEDITATION

Sufi meditation involves seeing one's spiritual guide by means of this second form of sight. It is the seeker's attempt to concentrate his thoughts on the screen of the mind, liberating his perceptions from physical limitations. The more frequently he is able to project a thought form upon that mental screen, the more vividly that mental pattern will be realized within the mind. That is why maintaining consistency is so important with this practice, and indeed with all spiritual practices.

Sufi meditation may then be seen as a mental approach whose ultimate goal is to allow the seeker to travel from this world of illusion to the Divine Presence. When we visualize our spiritual mentor, our Sufi spiritual master, the knowledge of the Divine Attributes that operate through him is reflected back upon our minds. With frequent repetition, the mind of the follower reaches the level of enlightenment, acquires the ability to communicate directly with the Guide, and acquires spiritual awareness of the Guide. In the science of Sufism, this state is referred to as the station of Affinity.

The best and most reliable way of enjoying this affinity is through the longing passion of love for the Guide. By maintaining the practice of meditation, the mind of the Guide continues to transfer knowledge and understanding to the mind of the follower, according to the intensity or degree of this love. As this love grows and the bond of Sufi meditation intensifies, the Divine Lights operating in and through the Guide—which are, in fact, reflections of the Beatific Vision of God— are transferred to the follower. This enables him to become familiar with the Lights of the Divine Presence, so that he can experience the Beatific Vision and open the doorway within his heart to the Presence of God. In Sufism, this state is referred to as the station of "Becoming One with the Guide."

These Lights and this Vision of the Divine Presence are not personal traits of the Guide. Just as the follower is able to experience these Divine Realities through his spiritual connection with the Guide, the Guide experiences them through his spiritual connection with the Holy Prophet ﷺ. The Guide, in his turn, absorbed the knowledge and attributes of the Prophet ﷺ through the same devoted attention and concentration. In the language of Sufism, this state of affinity between the shaykh and the Prophet ﷺ is referred to as the station of "Oneness with the Holy Prophet." And it is through this spiritual union with the Prophet ﷺ that the shaykh is able to share his abilities with the follower.

In the state of "Oneness with the Holy Prophet," the follower is gradually consumed by love, passion, and longing for the Prophet ﷺ until, step-by-step, he assimilates and apprehends the knowledge of the Prophet ﷺ. At that auspicious moment, the knowledge and learning of the Prophet ﷺ is transferred to the seeker in accordance with his capacity. He also absorbs the traits and attributes of the Holy Prophet ﷺ, again each according to his capacity, aptitude, and ability.

From this exalted state, the follower continues to progress by developing his affinity with the Prophet ﷺ. Ultimately, he reaches the point of being able to truly and authentically acknowledge the Lordship of God, recognizing God as the Lord of All the Worlds with full comprehension and acceptance of the meaning of that Lordship. At this point, he declares, "Yes, indeed, You are our Lord God!" This is the station of affinity with God, and is referred to in Sufism as the state of "Unique Oneness in the Divine Presence," or simply "Oneness."

Where the follower goes from this station—if he is granted the ability to reach it and continue beyond—is beyond the power of words to narrate or explain, for it is a realm of spiritual subtlety that cannot be described.

THE GUIDE: PORTAL TO THE DIVINE PRESENCE

The ultimate goal and purpose, then, of Sufi meditation is to maintain a perpetual presence in the reality of the Guide (shaykh). Therefore, the more one keeps to this vital practice, the more its benefits will manifest in his daily life until he reaches the state of annihilation in the presence of the Guide.

The Guide is the bridge between this world of illusion and the realm of reality. He remains in this world only for that purpose. The Guide is a rope thrown to those who seek freedom from this world, one that extends from this plane of unreality directly to the Divine Presence. Thus, to be annihilated in the presence of the spiritual master is to be annihilated in that Divine Presence, for the reality of his being is there.

The knowledge of this Way is always expanding. It is an ocean of wisdom that is always fresh, never stale. As our understanding increases, so does our ability to receive new information, to comprehend new knowledge, to reach even higher levels of understanding.

To be a traveler on this path is to be a diver into these oceans of sacred knowledge. When we only walk on the shores of this great sea, we may find a few seashells or polished stones. The real treasures, however, can be found only by diving. But we are not born swimmers. How, then, can we begin to explore the waters where secret treasures lie? The answer lies with our master, for only by following one who has already fathomed and charted these murky depths can we hope to find our way.

By taking the hand of the master—by taking initiation with him— you grab hold of a lifeline leading from the seashore down into that ocean of knowledge. In taking his hand, you are taking God's ﷻ hand and grabbing hold of the rope that is the only real safety for mankind.

These treasures lie in dark depths. At best, you may be able to bring a small lamp to light your way. But the master has a spotlight. If you journey into the darkness of these unknown regions with your small lamp, you might easily become lost. The master's light penetrates the darkness that hides the treasures and illuminates your way to them.

You can use the master's light by connecting your heart with his heart. This is referred to as the Noble Connection. In the Naqshbandi practice of *dhikr* (remembrance), the Guide may tell his followers to connect their hearts to the heart of the Prophet ﷺ, but this is said to avoid breaches of protocol, and is done out of humility. In reality, the direct connection to the Prophet's ﷺ heart is beyond you, the ocean of his knowledge is too vast. So you must say, "O Lord, connect my heart to one who is witnessing *Sayyidina* Muhammad ﷺ, because I am still blind."

You cannot travel directly to Presence of God, the Almighty and Exalted. In the Holy Quran, God tells believers to:

… Enter houses through their proper doors. (2:189)

The open meaning of this verse (which is obvious in the context of the entire verse) has to do with the abandonment of a superstitious practice associated with the new moon. But there is an esoteric meaning to the verse also, a commandment from God to approach Him with respect and humility through the correct procedures—not directly, but through the proper doorway. It means to seek His representative, and that is none other than the Prophet Muhammad ﷺ.

We would never brashly walk into a palace and demand an audience with the king. Rather we would attempt to follow the proper protocols, asking first to speak with the ruler's representative. Certainly, one should not dare to approach the Lord of All Creation with less deference.

Therefore we must seek out our Lord's representative, who is the Holy Prophet ﷺ. Here, too, we must approach with respect and enter through the proper door. And the door to the Prophet ﷺ is our shaykh.

SUFI MEDITATION AND OTHER TRADITIONS

There are elements of other spiritual traditions that may seem similar to Sufi meditation. That is because those traditions have taken from the secrets of Islamic meditation, even if unknowingly.

There are some people who have developed certain spiritual powers by following a different way of meditation or practicing a different spiritual philosophy. God is merciful, and is giving them something as a reward for their efforts.

And He has subjected to you, as from Him, all that is in the heavens and on earth. (45:13)

These other philosophies and spiritual paths all represent different ways of struggling against the self, but God does not give to others what He gives to His saints. He rewards the efforts of all, but He only gives them a portion of what He gives to believers. The topmost levels are not open to them; they can reach so far, but no more. Only through the perfection of faith can we hope to reach the highest stations.

THE SEEKER AND THE SOUGHT

Make your Sufi meditation. Dive into the ocean of divine knowledge. Make the night vigil prayer each night before *Fajr*. Then you will be making the journey to *Sayyidina* Muhammad 鬘, traveling to His kingdom, and standing before his door. When you arrive at that blessed door, imagine the Guide going before you. Then you can knock upon that door saying, "O Master, gaze upon me! Notice I am pounding on your door!"

In reality, we are non-existent. Each of us is nothing more than an atom. We must ask God to forgive us for forgetting this. Each breath that we take without remembering our Lord, who provided it for us, is wrong. Not praising Him in each breath is wrong. Our whole existence is wrong. We must ask God to forgive us for our heedlessness. We must pray, "O our Lord, for the sake of Your greatness, forgive me. Whatever I have done wrong, forgive me!"

If we do this with sincerity, how is God going to deny us the forgiveness we seek? When you seek forgiveness, you become completely empty, as clear as crystal.

SECTION TWO: CORE PRACTICES OF SUFI MEDITATION

Sufi meditation is the key and essence to spiritual development, for it is nothing other than the development of excellence, which is the highest level of spirituality as taught by Prophet Muhammad 鬘. It is the very annihilation of oneself in the presence of the Divine, in the light and reality of the Guide, who is in reality the disciple's source, and the origin of the light of his or her soul.

Sufi meditation is thus a return to one's true and perfected original self, about which Prophet Muhammad ﷺ said, "Humans are born in a natural state of purity." It is the fastest and most direct method for spiritual progress. Sufi meditation is flight to safety from one's lower self to God. It is emigration from the false identity this world has assigned the individual to the real identity that God has created and which exists in His Divine Presence.

Sufi meditation is the perfect method for the development of spiritual consciousness, the awakening of the heart, soul, and the mind's light—otherwise dormant. Sufi meditation is the denial of the senses which enslave one to this world. Through meditation, one may awaken to the true reality. Thus it is the essence of asceticism, and the necessary path for seekers of the truth, for those men of God who willfully and completely turn away from this world, who will not and cannot rest until they arrive at their divine destinations.

Sufi meditation is also the means of healing the body with the light of the Divine. It leads to purification of the blood and the development of mastery over one's electromagnetic energy field. It is the key to the process of alchemy whereby the light, energy, and electricity of the Divine Presence change the mercury of this world that poisons one's system into the gold of the blessed Prophetic Light.

Sufi meditation is reality. It is moving from slavery and bondage towards emancipation and freedom. In summary and essence, to practice Sufi meditation is to die to the world and awaken into reality. It is, therefore, the aim, goal, and purpose of all spiritual practice.

PREPARING FOR SUFI MEDITATION

1. TIMING

The ideal time for Sufi meditation—and indeed for spiritual endeavors in general—is at night, preferably after midnight. This is the time when the world is asleep, but the lovers and seekers of God are awake and traveling towards reality and their Divine destinations. The plane of consciousness is made clear when this world is veiled by night, and the chaotic world is at rest. That is when the mind and heart may operate most efficiently and effectively.

Sufi meditation is actually a state of heedfulness that must be constantly and perpetually maintained during the day. Those committed to this path seek to maintain a state of mindfulness in each breath, not forgetting their Lord for even a moment. This said, the quiet hours of the night are the best time to begin to develop this practice. Sufi meditation before midnight is very slow; after midnight, it is very fast.

2. PURIFICATION

Before beginning Sufi meditation, the seeker must first make ablution with the realization of its inner aspects, washing away the burdens and darkness of this world from mind and body, igniting and sealing the energy that lies in one's being. The extremities washed during ablution are your primary means of interacting with this world, and any taint left by that contact must be cleaned off. The seeker must also wash private parts with water after using the restroom.

For more information on the outer aspects of cleanliness in Islam, refer to a non-Wahhabi and non-Salafi manual from any of the four accepted schools of Islamic jurisprudence. The seeker must be careful in soliciting advice and in choosing his spiritual and religious reading, because his spiritual life can be lost if he heeds ignorant people who call him away from the spiritual path, even if those who call him away pull him only into dry religious practice and not into full-blown pursuit of worldly dissipation. Today's mosques are full of people who veil their pursuit for this world with the pretense of service to God. Most of today's "Islamic" governments also veil their political ambitions with the color of Islam, while actually causing immense harm to the religion and its people by their disregard and disdain for heavenly law; therefore beware of texts about Islam published by governments. One book which discusses many aspects of Islamic law and good conduct is Reliance of the Traveler. For the beginner the best approach is usually to learn slowly, not to try to completely change overnight or in the space of a few months. A great deal can be learned by associating with other seekers.

For more information on the inner aspects of ablution, see p. 120 *et seq.*

3. DRESS

Just as it is important to maintain the purity of your body, it is also important to maintain a proper physical appearance. The most direct method for establishing your identity as a traveler upon the path of self-purification is to adopt the correct outward appearance, abandoning the dress of worldliness and instead wearing the apparel of the next life. In doing so, you leave behind your old identity, that slave of the material world, and assert your true identity as a servant of the Divine.

The dress most conducive to spirituality is the clothing worn by *Sayyidina* Muhammad ﷺ, the traditional clothing worn by the prophets of God. The follower must wear his best traditional Islamic clothing. The ideal color is white, for it best deflects the negativity and bad energy of this world.

We must hold fast to all the elements of proper Islamic tradition. For men, this means wearing the turban, cloak, ring and natural Muslim perfume. It also means carrying the tooth-stick. Ladies must wear proper Islamic attire, with loose white clothing being the most preferable.

This is the honored dress of the ascetics and lovers of *Sayyidina* Muhammad ﷺ— who reject completely the illusion of this material world and want nothing to do with it, who fast day and night from it, and who will settle for nothing less than the perfection and truth of reality.

4. Place

You should set aside a small corner of your house for spiritual activity, a niche which will become blessed and charged with angelic light and presence. If possible, select a part of the house into which light cannot easily penetrate. Lay out a nice prayer carpet, orienting it in the direction of prayer. Place a candle or oil lamp before it in emulation of *Sayyidina* Musa 🕊 who, in seeking the presence of the Divine, traveled towards the Burning Bush. It is also recommended that you light either incense or a scented oil diffuser to attract angels and positive energy. Finally, you should keep a picture of your Guide nearby as a spiritual compass with which to align yourself and to facilitate the connection to his presence and reality.

When we speak of creating complete darkness in the meditation place, that means a complete absence of <u>physical</u> light. It does not mean an absence of spiritual light, for that is precisely what we are seeking in Sufi meditation. The best way to seek such spiritual light is to find a room that no physical light can enter. If you do not have access to such a place, then go to the lowest level of your home and cover yourself with a blanket so that you can perceive no light (if you do this then of course you will have to modify spiritual exercises involving candles—do not burn yourself).

5. The Prayer of Ablution

After performing your ablutions and preparing the place of meditation, begin Sufi meditation by praying two cycles of the prayer of ablution. Keep in your mind the purpose and meaning of the prayer, its movements and inner aspects. The perfection of prayer is in *Sayyidina* Muhammad 🕊—in the very state of his being. The actual movements correspond to the letters of his Divine name, "Ahmad." When standing, one is in the position of the letter *alif* (ﺍ). In bowing, the letter *hah* (ﺡ) is formed. Prostration represents the *mim* (ﻡ). And sitting is the *dal* (ﺩ).

One must seek to become one with the reality of the prayer, which is nothing other than the reality of *Sayyidina* Muhammad ﷺ.

6. INTENTION

After completing the prayer of ablution, one should state one's intention as prescribed by Grandshaykh 'Abdullah ن:

> I intend the forty (days of seclusion); I intend seclusion in the mosque; I intend seclusion; I intend isolation; I intend discipline (of the ego); I intend to travel in God's Path; I intend to fast for the sake of God in this mosque.

7. RECITATION

Begin by repeating the testimonial of faith three times, renewing your faith in God and His Prophet ﷺ,

> *Ashhadu an la ilaha illa-Allah, wa ashhadu anna Muhammadan Rasulallah* – I bear witness that there is no god except God, and I bear witness that Muhammad is the Messenger of God.

Then ask God for forgiveness, repeating between 100 and 200 times,

> *Astaghfirullah al-'Azeem wa atubu Ilayh* – I ask God's forgiveness and I repent to Him.

Next, recite the 112th Surah three times.

Then make the Gifting, the prayer for Shaykhs of the Naqshbandi Order: (See p. 136)

Then recite Suratu 'l-Fatiha one time.

Finally, call upon the shaykh using his spiritual name, seeking his support and searching for his spiritual presence, by repeating at least

200 times, *Madad ya Sayyidi madad al-haqq, Mawlana Shaykh Nazim.* Repeat this as much as necessary to establish a connection with the shaykh.

THE LEVELS OF SUFI MEDITATION

LEVEL ONE: MEETING THE SHAYKH IN THE REALM OF THE SPIRIT

The goal of the first level of Sufi meditation is to imagine yourself in the presence of the Sufi spiritual master, to give him greetings, to converse with him, and to build a relationship with him on a spiritual level.

After proceeding through the aforementioned preparatory steps, visualize yourself in the presence of the Shaykh. The operative word here is "visualize." Visualizing is not the same as imagining. When we imagine something, we create a fictional illusion in our mind. What we are concerned with here is reality, and you must know that the follower <u>is truly</u> in the continual presence of the Shaykh, on the plane of the spirit.

So visualize that reality, projecting it onto the screen of your mind. Keep your eyes closed. See the Shaykh through the eye of the heart.

Do not look for his face. Instead, concentrate on his aura, his spiritual form. When you begin to perceive the Shaykh's presence, give him greetings. It is important to maintain proper manners with the Shaykh during Sufi meditation, behaving exactly as you would if you were in the Shaykh's physical presence. Sit still, maintaining a position of respect—if it is not too difficult for you, kneel. If this is too difficult, then sit cross-legged. Remain fully conscious, fully awake, and fully aware of your connection with the Shaykh.

At this point, you may allow your soul to converse with the Shaykh. In so doing you define, build, and strengthen your relationship with his reality. Follow what the Shaykh reveals to your heart about spiritual matters. However, with regard to worldly matters, any inspiration you receive through Sufi meditation should be confirmed with the Shaykh before you act on it.

LEVEL TWO: CONNECTING YOUR HEART WITH THE HEART OF THE SHAYKH

After mastering the first level of Sufi meditation, your next goal is to build a spiritual connection between your heart and the Shaykh's.

To accomplish this, begin as before and visualize yourself in his presence. After greeting the Shaykh, ask permission to connect your heart to his light and his heart to your light. Imagine a ray of light extending from the Shaykh's heart to your heart and another extending from your heart to the Shaykh's. This creates a powerful spiritual connection.

Once this connection is established, recite your daily assigned practice of Remembrance of God (*dhikr*), taking care to maintain the connection between your heart and the Shaykh's throughout (See the Appendix for details of the daily devotional practices, *awrad,* and an explanation of its secrets).

LEVEL THREE: CONTROLLING THE BREATH

The goal of this exercise is to practice conscious breathing.

According to Grandshaykh 'Abdul Khaliq Ghujdawani ق:

The most important mission for the seeker in this Order is to safeguard his breath, and he who cannot safeguard his breath, it would be said of him, "he lost himself."

The name *Allah*, which encompasses the ninety-nine Names and Attributes, consists of four letters, *alif* (ا), *lam* (ل), *lam* (ل), and *hah* (ه): الله. The people of Sufism say that the absolute unseen Essence of God is expressed by the last letter, *hah* (ه).

Shah Naqshband ق said:

This Order is built on breath. So it is a must for everyone to safeguard his breath in the time of his inhalation and exhalation, and further, to safeguard his breath in the interval between the inhalation and exhalation.

Dhikr is flowing in the body of every single living creature by the necessity of its breath—even without will—as a sign of obedience, which is part of its creation. Through its breathing, the sound of the letter *hah* of the Divine Name *Allah* is made with every exhalation and inhalation, and it is a sign of the Unseen Essence serving to emphasize the Uniqueness of God. Therefore, it is necessary to be present with that breathing in order to realize the Essence of the Creator.

Safeguarding your breath from heedlessness will lead you to complete Presence, and complete Presence will lead you to complete Vision, and complete Vision will lead you to complete Manifestation of God's ninety-nine Names and Attributes. God leads you to the Manifestation of His ninety-nine Names and Attributes and all His other Attributes, because it is said, "God's Attributes are as numerous as the breaths of human beings."

It must be known by everyone that securing the breath from heedlessness is difficult for seekers. Therefore, we must safeguard it by seeking forgiveness. Seeking forgiveness will purify it and sanctify our breath and prepare us for the Real Manifestation of God everywhere.

To perform this meditation, prepare as you would for any other form of Sufi meditation. Take special care during ablution to ensure that your hands are clean. Make your meditation space as dark as possible. Play a recording of Quranic recitation, prayers on the Prophet ﷺ, *dhikr*, or some other soothing sound.

Take care to perform even the smallest details of this form of Sufi meditation, because they are the foundation of your meditation. Assume a kneeling position or sit cross-legged in the "Lotus Position." Close your eyes and mouth. Clench your teeth together—gently, not hard—and keep your tongue pressed firmly against the roof of your mouth. Inhale, then hold your breath to slow your heart rate and breathing.

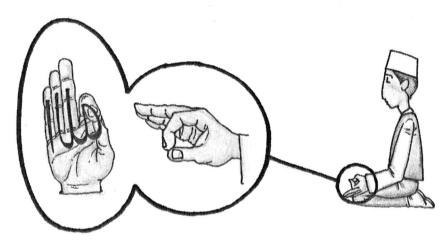

The hands carry tremendous secrets, and their position in this exercise is important. You will begin to unlock the secrets of the hands in this meditation. God placed Divine Codes on our hands—these are activated by rubbing them together (See page 120 *et seq.*). The hands can also function like satellite dishes, receiving Divine Energies and other emanations. Position your hands so that the tip of the thumb is touching the tip of the index finger, with the other fingers extended straight. This forms the shape of the word *Allah* in Arabic script.

Now pay attention to your breathing. Breathe in through your nose and exhale through your mouth. When you breathe in through your nose, say, *Hu-Allah.* Exhale through your mouth, saying *Hu.* As you breathe in, imagine white light entering through your heart. When you breathe out, imagine black energy being expelled from your mouth.

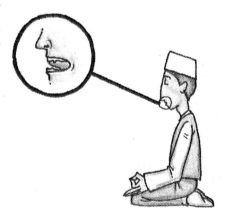

When we exhale, the carbon monoxide that leaves our bodies contains negative energy from our bad actions. Therefore the Prophet ﷺ said, "When you drink (water), do not breathe in the vessel."[1] When you visualize this bad energy leaving your body, these bad actions are being purged from your soul.

Grandshaykh Abdul Khaliq Ghujdawani ق said:

The wise seeker must safeguard his breath from heedlessness, coming in and going out, thereby keeping his heart always in the Divine Presence; and he must revive his breath with worship and servitude and dispatch this worship to His Lord full of life, for every breath which is inhaled and exhaled with Presence is alive and connected with the Divine Presence. Every breath inhaled and exhaled with heedlessness is dead, disconnected from the Divine Presence.

Keep repeating *Ya Sayyidi, ya sayyidi madad al-haqq, Mawlana Shaykh Nazim* while holding your index finger and thumb together gently and trying to feel your pulse. It is important to feel your own heart beating and make sure it is in tune with your breathing. Hear your heart beating, *Allah, Allah*. Remember that each of us is surrounded by a field of energy. You are receiving emanations of Divine Energy.

LEVEL FOUR: DRESSING YOURSELF IN THE LIGHT OF THE SHAYKH

Enter the presence of your Sufi spiritual master, then ask him to dress you in his light; to dress you in the divine dress that God has placed on him. Imagine the Shaykh's heart over your heart, his beard over your face. When you are dressed in the light of the Shaykh, it is as though you are wearing a favorite cloak of his. Keep repeating *Madad ya sayyidi madad al-haqq, Mawlana Shaykh Nazim, Madad Ya Sahibu'l-waqt.*

Remember, the Shaykh is with the Prophet ﷺ. The Shaykh is in the Divine Presence. He is one of those who died before they died. The

[1] Bukhari.

masters of this Order say we do not truly live until we die. We die by killing our desires. If we do this, then in every waking moment we will find ourselves in the presence of *Sayyidina* Muhammad ﷺ. But we are not yet at that station, and so we must attach ourselves to someone who is. By maintaining the Shaykh's light upon us and by continuing to see support by repeating *Madad ya sayyidi madad al-haqq, Mawlana Shaykh Nazim* throughout the day, we can maintain our connection with the Prophet ﷺ and the Divine Presence.

Consider the difference that this can make in our prayers. When we call *Allahu Akbar*, we must recognize that our prayer is of no importance to God. It is only important to us. We have an understanding of God, but we do not know His Reality. Nothing can occupy space with Him. Nothing can occupy that place except God. The only servant who truly understands that is the Prophet Muhammad ﷺ.

We cannot connect directly to Prophet ﷺ. We need a means, even if it is indirect, of connecting with God, and therefore we have to maintain our connection with our spiritual master who is connected to the Prophet ﷺ, who is connected with God. With this chain of connection, our prayer may mean something. And the same is true for *dhikr* or any other form of worship.

Visualize yourself being dressed with the light of the master, the light of his form. Imagine that your weak and deficient light bulb is suddenly being filled with his brilliant light. We are full of holes, so we cannot contain the light that enters into us and concentrate it. But the master's light is as bright as a laser. It is focused. And, as such, it is capable of transmitting enormous amounts of information.

Today, God has taught mankind to use lasers to beam data from one place to another. He is revealing this technology in order to show us that information is transmitted by light. This is the meaning of the term *Naqshbandi*. It refers to the ability to burn information into your heart and soul with light, just as a laser can burn data onto a compact disc.

As you visualize yourself being dressed in the light of the master, as you imagine his light filling you, pay attention to your breathing. Breathe in through your nose and, as you do, say *Allah* silently in your heart. Then breathe out through your mouth and, as you do, say *Hu*. As you do this, remain conscious of your heartbeat and maintain your connection with your shaykh, asking him to send more and more light into you.

That light will come and cauterize your deficiencies. Doctors used to use hot knives to sear the flesh they cut in order to stop the flow of blood, creating very strong scar tissue. The light of the master has a similar effect upon the spiritual body.

When we sin and fail to ask God for forgiveness, those sins become like barnacles or calluses on our souls. That is why the Prophet ﷺ used to say, "I see the scabs of devils." The master's light can burn away these impurities. The light of the Shaykh contains the light of his shaykh, which contains the light of the Prophet ﷺ. That is why it is so powerful.

Of course, our egos resist this purification. That is one of the reasons why it is so difficult to perform Sufi meditation. Another is that, in Sufi meditation, we are forced to examine ourselves and confront our mistakes and bad deeds head on. We are faced with the truth about ourselves.

During Sufi meditation, your Guide may ask you, "Why did you do this?" or "Why did you say that?" He may ask you to explain your actions, to examine your motivations and real intentions. In Sufi meditation, there is no hiding from the truth. Truth is coming and falsehood is vanishing. And we are not always happy with what we see.

Indeed, the ego will be very happy with its old station. It has no need to become a slave of the truth or a servant of the Prophet ﷺ. It has no need for such accounting. But we do, if we hope to advance upon the Path of Righteousness. We must practice Sufi meditation each night, reflecting upon our actions, and taking our due of praise or criticism from our shaykh; without such self-examination, we may spend our whole lives heedless of our bad actions.

If you can face such scrutiny, if you can break through the barriers thrown up by your ego to prevent this light from shinning in to the dark recesses of your soul, then whole oceans of knowledge and understanding will open up for you.

LEVEL FIVE: CARRYING THE DRESS OF THE SHAYKH

After we have built a strong connection between our heart and the heart of your spiritual teacher, the goal becomes to maintain that spiritual connection—not just in Sufi meditation, but throughout the day. There are three levels to this struggle: keeping the love for the Guide, keeping his presence, and making the Guide's will our will. This final level is that Station of Annihilation.

To accomplish this, you must wear the light of the Shaykh and, from this point forward, imagine that you are always cloaked in that spiritual raiment. You must not eat, drink, pray, perform *dhikr*, or do anything else without imagining the Shaykh's image upon you. Your love for the Shaykh will mix with his presence, and this will open the door to  annihilation in him. The more you can remain mindful of this spiritual dress, the more that you can remember to visualize it upon yourself throughout the day, the faster your progress towards that station will be and the more complete your annihilation in the Shaykh will become.

Once you have annihilated yourself in the presence of the Shaykh, he will annihilate you in the presence of the Holy Messenger of God, *Sayyidina* Muhammad ﷺ. Then you must keep the love of the Prophet ﷺ in your heart, just as you kept your love for the Shaykh. You must keep yourself in the presence of the Prophet ﷺ, just as you kept yourself in the presence of the Shaykh. And you must make the Prophet's ﷺ will your will, just as you executed the will of the Shaykh upon yourself.

This will lead you to the Divine Presence, to a station of being, yet being without existence—a clear vessel for whoever wishes to fill your being from God's Divine Kingdom. In this state of Oneness with *Sayyidina* Muhammad ﷺ, you gradually assimilate and understand his knowledge through passion, longing, and love.

DURATION OF SUFI MEDITATION

Initially, you may begin the practice of Sufi meditation for short intervals of five to fifteen minutes, and gradually work towards longer sessions. With practice, these sessions may extend for hours at a time. What is most important, however, is that you maintain a consistent practice, as this is the only way to gain any lasting benefit. It is better and wiser to perform Sufi meditation for a short time each day without omission than to be sporadic in your discipline and the practice thereof. If one applies a small amount of effort consistently, this will yield tremendous progress over time.

SECTION THREE: ADVANCED MEDITATIONS

PROPHETIC MEDITATION

Once the seeker has mastered the basic practice of Sufi meditation, he may move on to more advanced spiritual practices. In Prophetic Meditation, the seeker tries to build a personal relationship with the Prophet ﷺ.

To perform this exercise, you will need a cassette or compact disc recording of blessings on the Prophet ﷺ. Begin by dressing yourself with the light of the Shaykh. That is the first step for all of the more advanced forms of meditation. Close your eyes and visualize yourself in the presence of the master, dressed in his light. Then begin playing the recorded blessings. As you listen to the recorded blessings, you must know that the Prophet ﷺ is within you.

We all know that Satan is with us, always trying to ensnare us in his traps and whispering his lies in our ears. But *Sayyidina* Muhammad ﷺ is with us, too, and God gave more power to *Sayyidina* Muhammad ﷺ than He did to Satan. Our sultan is *Sayyidina* Muhammad ﷺ. So, as we believe in the presence of evil, we must believe in the even more powerful presence of his goodness.

In this meditation, you focus on that Prophetic presence within you. You must know it, feel it, see it, and you must say, "I am weak, I am poor, and *Sayyidina* Muhammad ﷺ is everything. Gaze upon me! Accept me to be in front of your Holy Grave! I am asking for your love, for your forgiveness, for your guidance, and for faith. That love you have for God, if you give me one drop of it I will drown! If you do not open your door, I am losing myself! Negativity is going to rip apart my faith! They are going to rip apart my family! Please, open your door!" You must pound on that door, the door of the Prophet ﷺ. And, when that door opens, you must place your head on the Prophet's ﷺ lap. Know that you are in his spiritual presence. Dress yourself in that holy presence and go into that holy heart, the Heart of Muhammad (s).

REACHING THE DIVINE PRESENCE: MEDITATION ON PROPHET MOSES

This form of meditation is best performed after midnight. To prepare for this meditation, you must first turn off the lights, thereby eliminating visual distractions and closing off that channel to this world. Once in the dark, imagine that you are in the grave and that this moment is the last moment before you leave this world. Imagine how you will feel at that moment. You are so in need of help. You are desperate for someone—anyone—to help you. At that moment, you must direct your heart to the helper that is nearest to you, and that is your master.

Of all the people you know, the shaykh is the nearest to the Prophet ﷺ, so you must direct your heart to him and, through him, to *Sayyidina* Muhammad ﷺ. This is the channel through which Divine aid can reach you in this moment of greatest need.

At this moment, you must also remember God's words about Prophet Moses ﷺ:

> *Behold, he saw a fire: So he said to his family, "Tarry ye; I perceive a fire; perhaps I can bring you some*

burning brand from it, or find some guidance at the fire." (20:10)

The phrase "*I perceive a fire*" can also be translated as "I looked, and felt a familiarity with something glowing there."

He said to his people, "I am going to go and see what kind of fire is there. I might be able to get some of it for my people in order to illuminate our way, or may find by its light some guidance." It means that he was asking to send that energy back to his family. The fire represents energy. God is showing that there was energy there, and that Prophet Moses ﷺ felt familiarity with the energy. He felt as if that energy was possessing him, overtaking him, compelling him to go to it and use it as a guide for himself and his people.

The Holy Quran then states:

But when he came to the fire, a voice was heard: "O Moses! Verily I am thy Lord! Therefore (in My presence) put off thy shoes: thou art in the sacred valley, Tuwa." (20:11-12)

When Prophet Moses ﷺ reached that energy, God said to him, "Take off your shoes." Physically this represents cleanliness for worship. On a spiritual level, God is commanding us to remove anything that relates to worldly life. A deeper spiritual meaning lies in the fact that at that time shoes were made from the hides of the most stubborn and ignorant of animals, donkeys. Therefore on a spiritual level God is ordering us to remove our own ignorance and to leave our egos. If we leave behind ego and ignorance, we may proceed into the light; dress ourselves in its energy, travel through that holy fire and reach the holy valley.

After leaving all ignorance and dirtiness of the selfish ego, then bathing in the healing energy, we must listen to what is revealed to us.

I have chosen thee: listen, then, to the inspiration (sent to thee). (20:13)

The Prophet Moses ﷺ was entering into a sort of meditation—a communion with the Divine Presence. Through it, he was looking for something by which to guide himself, his family and his people. He was directing and focusing his mind and body towards that Divine Energy that appeared as fire. As he directed himself towards that Divine Presence, God guided him. When he disconnected himself from this world, putting aside ignorance and arrogance, God said, "Listen to what is going to be revealed to you."

That is why we must begin this form of meditation by creating the right environment, one that approximates the conditions alluded to in these verses of Holy Quran. When we enter meditation, we must begin by entering, symbolically, into a space of physical darkness. This was the environment in which Prophet Moses ﷺ found himself. Prophet Muhammad ﷺ also used to enter this physical environment when he retreated into the Cave of Hira. It is that same complete darkness that we must emulate when we wish to enter into meditation.

The seeker's goal is to reach, spiritually, out of that darkness and find a source of illumination, a source of positive energy that offers enlightenment and guidance to that holy valley, that holy land which is the Divine Presence. We have to find this light and establish a strong connection with the Divine Presence. Then we can return to our families and communities with the energy and inspiration to heal, feed and water those who hunger and thirst for spiritual knowledge and guidance.

Now that you have created the proper environment, the next step is to place an oil lamp or candle before you, in the direction of prayer (the *qiblah*). Use a candle with a nice scent. If you must cover yourself with a blanket to achieve the necessary darkness, then do not use fire—do not risk burning yourself.

Every fragrance has a level of spiritual understanding associated with it. Not all scents are the same. That is why, when saints pass, people sometimes notice a nice fragrance in the room. Every saint has a different scent. Instead of sweat, fragrance comes from them. Perfume comes from their bodies because of their love, their passion, for God. That deep, burning love creates that beautiful smell. Today, in the West, we see people practicing what they refer to as "aromatherapy." This is based on knowledge they took from the saints of God. It is a secret of sainthood that has been given to western people.

Therefore, it is best for the seeker to select a scented candle or fragrant oil according to what the Shaykh has prescribed for him. Not everyone will benefit from the same smell in the same way. At the beginning level, however, it is all the same, so select a pleasing fragrance and know that, as you progress to a different level of spiritual awareness, you will need to find the corresponding scent. That is because each smell attracts a different level of understanding, and at each level of understanding, there is a different saint sitting with the key to that station. Each of these saints is under the Sultan of saints, and that one is facing the Golden Brick which is the Prophet ﷺ.

The candle or lamp that you place in front of you symbolizes the energy that Prophet Moses عليه السلام saw. As you sit before it, contemplating that light and smelling the fragrance emanating from it, imagine that you are reaching that holy valley in the last moment of your life. Imagine that you are passing towards the afterlife, concentrating all of your being on asking God to forgive you. Concentrate all of your feelings, all of your emotional energy on seeking your Lord's forgiveness.

When you are in that position of drawing your last breath, at the end of your time, at that last moment, begging the Lord Almighty for forgiveness, begin to recite the Prophet's ﷺ prayer for the blind man.

Oh God, I ask You and turn to You through my Prophet Muhammad, the Prophet of mercy; Ya Muhammad, I seek your intercession with my Lord for the return of my eyesight.

With that prayer, seeking by means of the Prophet ﷺ that God restore our spiritual vision, connect your heart—following that pleasant fragrance that is coming to you, focusing your vision upon that flickering flame—to the light that is there. Open your eyes and focus on that light. Everything else is dark; only that light is there. Look at that light, maintaining a clear and unwavering focus on it for five minutes. Do not move or look aside. Concentrate your gaze upon that flame for five minutes.

Then close your eyes and keep them closed for five minutes, concentrating now upon the image of your shaykh. Concentrate on his image, imagine that he is connecting you to the heart of the Prophet ﷺ. Visualize yourself holding the hand of your master, and imagine that he is taking you into the presence of *Sayyidina* Muhammad ﷺ.

After five minutes, open your eyes again, visualizing now that the Prophet ﷺ is guiding your master—and you behind—into the holy valley. Wait for inspiration to come into your heart, again maintaining this attitude for five minutes.

Approximate the five minutes. There is no need to look at your watch.

Once you reach the point of feeling yourself in the presence of the master, connecting your heart to his heart, you must recite *Astaghfirullah* for approximately two-and-a-half minutes. Then call upon the Shaykh, repeating, *Ya Sayyidi* for the remainder of that five-minute period. Each time you repeat this phrase, you must pause and meditate upon it. When you say, *Ya Sayyidi,* you are with the Shaykh.

Then, when you begin the journey to the presence of the Prophet ﷺ, you must call upon him, either by repeating blessings on him or by repeating, *Ya Rasul-Allah, Ya Sayyid, Ya Sahib, Ya Siddiq, Ya Rasul, Ya Allah!* Again, you must pause and meditate upon each phrase. When you say, *Ya Sayyid,* you are with the Shaykh. When you say, *Ya Sahib,* you are with *Sayyidina* Mahdi ؏. When you say, *Ya Siddiq,* you are with *Sayyidina* Abu Bakr ⬧. When you say, *Ya Rasul*, you are with the Prophet ⬧). And when you say, *Ya Allah*, it is as if you are walking towards Him, walking into the Divine Presence with the help of the Prophet ⬧ and your shaykh.

When you finally reach to the last station of this meditation—the station of the Divine Presence—you must say, *Ya Allah*, once again pausing to meditate upon that phrase each time you repeat it.

The first time you perform this meditation, you might not reach all the way to the end, or hear any inspiration if you do. Do not be discouraged by this. If you perform this meditation every day, without interruption, for forty days, you will be able to receive some kind of inspiration through your heart. However, if you miss a day, you will have to maintain this practice for another forty days.

If you keep up this practice, you will, day-by-day, find yourself more and more able to visualize the shaykh. It will be as though you are seeing him before you, even though your eyes are closed. Then you will begin to feel the presence of the Prophet ⬧. You may not see him, but you will feel his presence. Once you do, then you can begin to feel the Divine Presence there, too.

As you move forward slowly, these feelings will gradually increase. They might develop quickly if you try hard and increase the time you spend in this meditation, adding another five minutes, another five minutes, another five minutes until you find yourself able to do it for a half an hour, an hour, or more. Each seeker must progress according to his or her ability. And, as always, it is better to maintain constantly a small amount rather than to maintain erratically a large amount of meditation.

The journey to this station is one that requires tremendous spiritual and physical work. Sufi meditation requires both spiritual and physical exertion because you are trying to control your body as well your mind. You are trying to sever your body's ties to this world, to prevent your body from being involved with its many distractions. You are trying to bring your body into the circle of the spirit, to bring it into the light of that holy energy, that source of illumination and guidance.

Once you reach that point, you will receive guidance—and you must listen to the guidance that you receive, to the inspiration that is being received through your heart, for with this guidance you will be able to be of help to those around you. Each person will receive different inspirations, different information, different instructions for healing themselves and others of spiritual or physical sicknesses.

This meditation, if performed diligently and consistently, will open the door to more physical and spiritual power for the seeker. It is an important step that you must take and master before continuing on to higher level exercises. By mastering this practice, you learn how to tap into powerful energies. Later practices teach the seeker how to use those energies for physical and spiritual healing. If you are successful here, then you may continue on to the next stage.

SECTION FIVE: CONCLUSION

To climb the mountain, the seeker must journey from the lower world to the Divine Presence. He or she must travel from the ego's world of sensual reality to the soul's world of Divine reality.

To make progress on this journey, we must bring into our heart the picture of the Shaykh, as it is the most powerful means of detaching ourselves from the hold of the senses. The Shaykh becomes, in our hearts, the mirror of the Absolute Essence. If we are successful in this, we reach the state of self-effacement—absence from the world of the senses. To the degree that this state increases in us, our attachment to the world of the senses will weaken and disappear, and we will come into the Station of the Absolute Void—not sensing anything other than God.

The highest degree of this station is called Annihilation. Thus, Shah Naqshband ق said:

> The shortest path to our goal, which is God, Almighty and Exalted, is for God to lift the veil from the Essence of the Face of His Oneness that appears in all creation. He does this with the State of Erasure and Annihilation in His Absolute Oneness, until His Majestic Essence dawns upon and eliminates the consciousness of anything other than Him. This is the end of the Journey of Seeking God and the beginning of another Journey.

At the end of the Journey of Seeking and the State of Attraction comes the State of Self-Effacement and Annihilation. This is the goal of all mankind as, God mentioned in the Quran:

> *I did not create Jinn and Mankind except to worship Me.* (51:56)

Chapter
2

Divine Energy

Divine Energy

Section One: The Nature of Divine Energy

*D*ivine Energy is the life breath transmitted to us from God. This energy regulates our thought patterns and emotions, is the source of our life force, and is the animating factor in all living beings. It is the stuff from which the constituent components of atoms are made. It gives life to every cell and motion to every galaxy. It is the source of all movement in the universe.

Divine Energy, which may also be referred to as "cosmic energy" or "the universal force," includes the energies of the stars, planets, and galaxies. This vast, all-pervading force nourishes the soul and spirit, and is the wellspring of energy that is in every living creature. This energy is never lost and exists without the secret of its nature being understood by science or modern medicine.

In different cultures, Divine Energy is known by different names: *Ki* in Japanese, *Chi* in Chinese, *Prana* in Hindi, *Qudra* in Arabic.

This Divine Energy circulates through our bodies and can be harnessed for healing. When the human body dies, the original life force—the Divine Energy that is within the body—leaves it and allows the body to decompose. The body goes back to its earthen origins and the spirit returns to its angelic origin of the Divine Energy from which it is composed.

Divine Energy, then, is nothing less than the animating force of this universe—and every universe. Its power is real, active, and continuous. Without it, nothing would live, nothing would exist. With it, all the amazing feats of life become possible, from the development of the human embryo from a microscopic clot, to the sundering apart of a huge block of concrete by a tiny seedling in an industrial wasteland.

In the human body, this Divine Energy impels every organ and drives every cell. When the body's life force diminishes, the anatomic relations of the body's organs are altered and disrupted, which leads to pain, organ dysfunction, and an overall deterioration of health. The Divine Energy within the body interacts with the Divine Energy that is everywhere around it, creating an electromagnetic field around itself. Thus, Divine Energy not only animates the body, but also gives it identity.

JRCE OF DIVINE ENERGY

Energy. Divine Energy is like the energy
, is fueled by nuclear fusion. In a fusion
ome together to form a single nucleus.
ass is lost from the original atoms, and
to the formula $E=MC^2$. C is the speed of
juare is even more immense; therefore a
ed. Also, the effect on one atom has an
ting a chain reaction. Fusion reactions
r stars become self-sustaining and can
of years.

s use both fusion (joining atoms) and
Earth, these abominations kill millions
in which they are detonated. On the
the same process of nuclear reaction continues on and on, giving
immense benefit to the people of Earth. So what is the difference?
Everything related to the heavens gives benefit, while everything on the
Earth is cursed. That is why the tremendous energy of nuclear reactions
gives death and destruction on Earth.

On Earth, the detonation of a nuclear bomb is an evil thing because
of the terrible destruction and loss of life that it causes. All evil has to
fade to nothingness, and truth has to continue. So this is why the effect
of a nuclear bomb, while terrible, is only temporary.

It is proof enough of the miraculous nature of God's creation that
nuclear explosions are happening every day and every moment on the
sun and yet the sun continues existing for millions of years. If one
big nuclear explosion happened on Earth, the entire planet would be
broken into small pieces.

The Power of the Sun

Everything that we see on Earth benefits from the sun's energy. This is the glory of the sun, for it is always sending its rays out to nourish, sustain and give life to  this world and to everything on it and in it. Scientists are only just beginning to understand how deeply the sun's radiation penetrates into the ground and how, even in the darkest caves, its energy is giving and sustaining life.

The sun gives life to plants, animals and human beings. Without it, none of these would exist. But we must ask ourselves, "To Whom does the sun belong?" The sun did not create itself. Rather, it was created and fixed in its place by the One who created all things. It was ordered to be there, and so it is and so it will remain until its being is ordered to cease.

But the sun emits more than light and heat and radiation. It also sends forth heavenly knowledge in the form of Divine Codes. And the codes that it is sending forth today are not the same as the codes it was sending yesterday. The codes that it sends tomorrow will be different still, because the sun has been programmed by the One who fixed it there.

Therefore, even the sun—with all of its power and glory—is nothing but an expression of the will of the One who created it. God uses the sun, our star, to send light to this world, and to send Divine codes.

GOOD AND EVIL ENERGY IN HUMAN BEINGS

Evil energy has been building up in our bodies as a result of our sins, and the negative energy that we generate attracts more and more evil energy, from the bad people we associate with and from evil beings that are all around us. Those evil beings are capable of generating a tremendous amount of negative energy, and this dark energy is attracted to other dark energy. This negative energy becomes like a shield around a person, engulfing him like a dark cloud through which little or no light can penetrate.

This barrier is like the heat shield on a spacecraft. The space shuttle, for example, is covered with special heat-resistant tiles that protect it from the tremendous heat generated when it reenters Earth's atmosphere. That fire is so intense that, if even one of these tiles is missing, the whole spacecraft will simply disintegrate and burn up, as we saw so tragically in 2003.

Scientists have created this impervious shield to protect their spacecraft. In the same way, many of us have built an impervious shield of negative energy around us. For many, the construction of this barrier began in childhood, with our childish ego. As we grow up, many of us continue to act childishly, thereby adding to this barrier of negativity. We build it up with arrogance and pride, and it then leads us to lie, cheat, forget saints, forget the Prophet ﷺ, and to forget God.

This leads many to lose faith.

Some people say, "We are not achieving any spiritual growth in our lives. We feel distracted. We are praying and making Sufi meditation, but nothing is happening. We are losing confidence in ourselves. We are losing faith."

These are good people, honest in confessing that they are losing faith. In doing so, they are saying that they want their faith back. All of us lose faith, because Satan is running after each of us and trying to take it away from us. There are other people who have no belief in spirituality. Many of them find that their worship has no taste. They have no longing for the Prophet ﷺ or for saints. They long only for this world and for bad actions. For them, religion becomes a bitter burden that they bear only grudgingly, if at all.

Therefore, admitting that one is losing confidence or faith is a good thing, because the first step to remedying a problem is to acknowledge it. At that point of admission that the problem exists, the process of healing can begin. And that process begins with initiation (baya').

When a person suffers kidney failure, doctors prescribe dialysis to purify his blood. Knowing that this procedure must be repeated regularly, the doctor begins by putting a tube into the patient's arm so they will not have to make a new puncture in the arm every time the patient must undergo dialysis. After that tube is installed, whenever the doctor wants he can just hook the patient up to the dialysis machine and it will begin to clean the body.

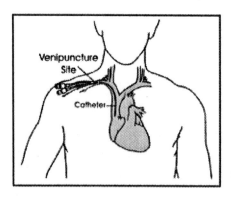

When you take initiation, it is as though the Shaykh inserted such a tube into your heart. Your spiritual connection with the Shaykh is like a catheter through which he can inject spiritual medicine in specific doses at specific times in your life. This tube also penetrates the shield of negative energy that surrounds you, allowing positive energy—Divine Energy—to enter your body. Once it does, that shield will begin to break down.

It is for this reason that God said:

> *... and indeed you have already known the first form of creation (that is the form of Adam). Why then do you not then take heed?* (56:62)

In this verse, God is saying that He created mankind perfect without any pollution, and is asking why we fail to remember that. God continues by saying,

> *Then tell me about the seed that you sow in the ground.* (56:63)

The meaning of this verse is, "Tell me about the seed that you have grown in your body. What kind of plant have you planted there? Does it bear good fruit or bad fruit? Are you generating good energy or polluted energy?"

If we are generating polluted energy, then we must recognize that we are in error, that we have made a mistake. Whatever you have intended in life is what you have planted. If your intention was good, then your plant will bear good fruit and generate positive energy. If your intention is bad, then your plant will bear evil fruit and generate negative energy.

God also asks:

> *Is it ye that cause it to grow, or are We the Cause? Were it Our Will, We could crumble it to dry powder.* (56:64-65)

If you put that dark shield up around yourself and keep it up, then you are going to regret it. You will see nothing through your heart, for your heart will be shrouded in darkness. However, if you allow that shield to be penetrated and destroyed by the Divine Energy that streams through that heavenly channel, then you will find what you are looking for.

Every person has a channel. Every human being has his own channel that God gave to them, and that channel is for him and nobody else. The only one who can guide you to your channel is the spiritual doctor who inserted his catheter into your heart. Without that first insertion, you will not be able to break through that shield of negative energy. That doctor has to find the weak spot in your barrier and punch through it. Only then can the heavenly serum of Divine Energy flow into your heart and begin dissolving the cloud of darkness.

The only way to maintain the flow of that Divine Energy is through Sufi meditation.

Meditation is like a magnifier. If you put a piece of paper out in the sun, it will not burn. But if you hold a magnifying glass over it and focus the sun's rays upon that paper, it will quickly ignite and burn. In the same way, Sufi meditation focuses the waves of Divine Energy into your heart and burns away the negative energy that accumulates around you. That is the only way to destroy the shield that Satan and your ego have built around you.

DIFFICULTIES: THE FUEL OF THE SOUL

Everyone wants to be on the Straight Path, for that is the way that leads to the Presence of God. However, many are distracted from that Path, and distraction leads to another way, a way which may not end in the Divine Presence. Indeed, those who are distracted may find themselves hopelessly lost, and may fail ever to reach that most sublime of goals. That is why God sends His prophets, His messengers, and the Seal of Messengers—to show us the right Way, to help us understand how to walk it, and to heal all the pain and sadness that may occur in our lives.

Pain and sadness are important, because they remind us to watch our steps and not to lose the Way. When you experience difficulty, you remember God. When you are in pain, you remember God. When you feel sadness, you remember God. When you are sick, you remember God. When you are lonely, you remember God. When you are longing for someone that you love, you remember God. And it is through this remembrance that we advance upon the Path to God.

That is how the saints were able to reach such high levels of spiritual development, because they were always longing to reach their Creator, and longing to reach the door of Prophet Muhammad ﷺ. They wanted to reach Prophet's ﷺ door because they knew that it led to the Door of God. This, also, is why they obeyed their spiritual guides, because they knew that whatever they told them was from the Prophet ﷺ and whatever was from the Prophet ﷺ was from God. Therefore they did not care whether their master's orders would cause them difficulty, for they knew that whatever the Shaykh was telling them had no purpose other than to pull their souls back to the Divine Presence. Whatever they suffered as a result was for the sake of their Lord.

And so it must be for the sincere follower. He must understand that whatever his Guide tells him is coming from the Prophet ﷺ and, ultimately, from God Himself. He must know that whatever the Shaykh orders him to do is for his benefit, for his spiritual advancement, and that whatever difficulty or hardship he may suffer as a result will only bring him closer to his Lord, which is the goal of all spiritual effort.

When we encounter difficulties along the Way, we burn as if consumed by fire, and our souls flee to the refuge of our Prophet ﷺ where we know our hearts will find peace. When we are faced with such trials, overwhelming energy is generated within the heart and spreads throughout the entire body. When we suffer loss or separation, the pain we suffer reminds us of the importance of that love, and that may in turn remind us of the love of the Shaykh, the love of the Prophet ﷺ, and the love of God.

God said in the Holy Quran:

If they had only, when they were unjust to themselves, come unto thee and asked God's forgiveness, and the Messenger had asked forgiveness for them, they would have found God indeed Oft-returning, Most Merciful. (4:64)

When we oppress ourselves, we may find ourselves in a situation that makes us remember the love of the Prophet ﷺ, that makes us come to the door of Prophet Muhammad ﷺ just as the Companions came, saying, "*Ya Rasulullah!*" and seeking forgiveness. God made this a condition of forgiveness, and He ordered the Prophet ﷺ to ask forgiveness on their behalf. This was the means through which they were able to reach the Divine Presence.

This is why spirituality is very important, because spirituality—which is the process of seeking the state of excellence by struggling against the ego—is the way that leads people to the Divine Presence.

If the love the saints have for the Prophet ﷺ were revealed, it would burn. When that love comes, they cannot control themselves. They are overcome with tears. That love for the Prophet ﷺ is beyond description. That kind of energy can burn every other kind of energy. That kind of energy can overcome every other kind of energy. And that kind of energy brings such tears to their eyes as could bring fire down from heaven. When you have that kind of love for the Prophet ﷺ, you will be filled with that energy and, when you come into his presence, that energy will burn away all the veils that separate you from him. Then you can make meditation with the Prophet ﷺ face-to-face, directly, and without anything separating you from him.

That is the experience the shaykhs of this Order reach through their seclusions, and that is their experience in life. That is why they are so full of praise for the Prophet ﷺ. That comes from the emotions of a burning heart. If their tears were turned into ink and their hairs into pens, they would write all kinds of praises, describe all kinds of beauty, compose all kinds of blessings, and reveal all kinds of revelations that God has thrown into their hearts. Every tear, every hair, every drop of blood coursing through their veins and capillaries would be writing *Muhammadun Habibullah, Muhammadun Rasulullah, Muhammadun Khaliullah, Muhammadun Naji'ullah* ﷺ.

Chapter
3

Angelic Healing

Chapter

3

Angelic Healing

SECTION ONE: INTRODUCTION TO ANGELIC HEALING

*M*astering Sufi meditation is the first step in developing one's healing abilities. It is the necessary foundation upon which all of the more advanced exercises are built. After a person masters Sufi meditation, he or she will have access to the physical and spiritual powers needed to heal diseases and ailments of the spirit and of the body. The methods for using these energies are discussed in this chapter. It is, therefore, essential that the seeker establish proficiency in the various forms of meditation before moving on to the practice of healing.

THE SCIENCE OF ANGELIC HEALING

The angelic healing process rejuvenates the body's life force and strengthens it through several focal points located throughout the body. On a biological level, spiritual exercises produce a neuro-psychological effect—causing the central nervous system to produce a carefully orchestrated endocrine response that relieves pain, heals the diseases of affected areas, and balances the entire body. On a spiritual level, the effects are even more profound.

Physicians and scientists are all acquainted with this unquantifiable life force, but are unable to interact with it directly except through its vehicle, the physical body. For that reason, scientists focus on the physical vehicle and invent procedures and techniques to keep the body in homeostasis, striving to keep the vital life force in the body as much as possible and to keep the body free of pain.

Therefore, the contemporary physician is concerned primarily with the physical body and, secondarily, with the psychological aspects of human existence. Therapies for illness are largely physical, whether in the form of medication, surgical intervention, or the like. Spiritual healers, on the other hand, use an inward approach to healing, by applying spiritual techniques and methods to cure the body on an energy level. The difference is that the spiritual healer heals from the inside out, while the physician heals from the outside in. Each is doing good for their patients and both meet on the common ground of curing disease and relieving pain and suffering.

Angelic healing is accomplished through the use of Divine Energy. Through the practice of Sufi meditation, one learns how to tap into this energy. In healing, one channels this energy and administers it for curative or therapeutic purposes. The primary tool used by the angelic healer is not a syringe or a scalpel, but the hands—for it is through the hands that this heavenly power is collected, focused, and released.

Energy can also be released through the feet, though this is of limited use in healing. The feet are only used in treating back problems, but here they can be potent tools if used by one who has understanding. Those who are descendants of the Prophet ﷺ are especially effective at healing backaches or other back problems with their feet, provided they have the proper training.

In general, however, healing is done with the hands. There are certain positions of the fingers and ways of touching and feeling that allow the healer to effect a cure. The healer must know how to open the hands in particular ways, how to collect, manage and release the energy they have concentrated, directing this energy at the source of the ailment.

This is a fundamental principle of the science of Islamic healing. One can also see it being applied by those who have borrowed from those teachings, like the followers of the Eastern mystical traditions.

In Buddhism, for example, we see the hands used as a means of releasing energy from the body. Practitioners of that tradition collect energy through their bodies in the same way that a parabolic dish collects energy from a satellite. Through different movements and stressful physical exercises, some Buddhists begin to acquire that kind of energy, concentrate it, and then release it through their hands into the bodies of sick people. The Buddhists use these techniques without knowing that they are Islamic secrets.

These are not superstitious practices. They <u>can</u> have an effect. Such energy, properly channeled and focused, can heal—just as a laser can be used in the hands of a contemporary physician to heal. Today, for example, it is routine to use a laser to heal diseases of the eye, even to cure blindness. Doctors no longer use knives or needles in such procedures. Instead, they use energy in the form of laser light.

ORIGINS OF ISLAMIC HEALING

The prophets of God taught their peoples several healing methods. These methods have been passed down from generation to generation and form the basis of most traditional medicinal practices. In the Islamic tradition, healers have relied on both physical and spiritual means that together constitute the science known as prophetic medicine.

Prophetic medicine is based on solid scientific principles, many of which are only now becoming known in the West. On a spiritual level, prophetic medicine employs techniques that utilize Divine Energy, often invoked through recitations, devotions, supplications, and meditation—all means taught by the prophets, messengers, and saints. But prophetic medicine does not ignore physical remedies. Rather, it is a holistic system designed to cure disease and to promote physical and spiritual wellness.

After curing a patient through spiritual means, the Prophet Muhammad ﷺ was once asked whether medicines should also be used by healers. "Yes," he said, "you must seek remedy from medicine, because whatever disease God has created in this world, He has created its remedy—except for the one disease with no remedy, old age."

Each prescribed Quranic verse has its own unique healing property which differs from those of other verses. The following are some examples of verses used in spiritual healing:

Six Quranic Verses of Healing: Ayat Al-Shifa

"And [God] shall heal the breast of the believers."

(wa yansurkum 'alayhim wa yashfi sudoora qawmin mumineena) (9:14)

"Mankind there has come to you a guidance from your Lord and a healing for (the diseases) in your hearts, and for those who believe a guidance and a mercy."

(Yaa ayyuha an-naasu qad ja'atkum maw'ithatun min rabbikum wa shifaun limaa fee as-sudoori wa hudan wa rahmatun lil-mumineen) (10:57)

"There issues from within the bodies of the bee a drink of varying colors wherein is healing for mankind."

(yakhruju min butooniha sharaabun mukhtalifun alwaanuhu feehi shifaun lin-naas) (16:69)

"And We sent down in the Quran such things that have healing and mercy for the believers."

(Wa nunazzilu mina al-qurani ma huwa shifaun wa rahmatun lil-mumineen) (17:82)

"And when I am ill, it is [God] who cures me."

(Waitha maridtu fahuwa yashfeeni) (26:80)

A supplication of Prophet Abraham

"And declare (O Muhammad) that [the Quran] is a guidance and healing for the believers."

(qul huwa lil-ladheena amanoo hudan wa shifaun) (41:44)

PREPARING TO HEAL

Before you can become an effective healer, you must first declare war on your ego. When you struggle against the ego and fight against its desires, you are exercising your spiritual power. The use of that spiritual power to contradict and check the ego causes that power to increase.

The principle is the same one used in contemporary fitness training. Athletes use resistance training to strengthen their bodies. By struggling against weights, they increase the strength of their bodies. In the same way, we increase our spiritual strength by struggling against our egos.

Moreover, as we make progress in this struggle, we dispel the negative energy that is generated by our egos and our bad desires. As that negative energy decreases, the positive energy around us increases.

Section Two: Sufi Keys to Health

Before you can master the art of healing, you must first understand the sources of disease and the means of maintaining good health. Though the complete system of prophetic medicine is beyond the scope of the present text, it is important to consider a few key principles of Islamic medical philosophy.

The Importance of Diet

Eating pure and lawful food (*halal*) is an essential part of maintaining the purity of one's blood. *Halal* literally means "permissible" or "lawful," the opposite of *haram*, forbidden, but in the context of diet it means to observe the strict guidelines of Islamic Divine Law (*Shariah*) in the selection and slaughter of meat. Making sure to consume only lawful food is essential to spiritual progress. Of course, making sure that every piece of meat one consumes is lawful can be difficult these days. Some people find it too difficult. If the burden is too great for you to bear, then eat what you like. But if you take this path of eating what you like, do not be surprised if it hampers your spiritual progress.

Those who wish to advance quickly upon this path must take great care with regard to their food. For them, it is not enough to make sure that their food is lawful; they must also consider who is preparing the food that they are eating.

The Companions of the Prophet ﷺ said that they refrained from seven-eighths of what is lawful out of fear of coming near to what is prohibited (*haram*). They did this because they realized the full implications of their actions and wanted to uphold more than the letter of the law. They sought to arrive at their divine destinations by means of assiduous performance and omission of actions in order to stay well within both the letter and the spirit of the law.

The masters of the Naqshbandi Order are very strict. Masters of previous times cared so much about this issue that they sometimes prepared their own food, or ate no food at all in order to perfect and purify themselves. Moreover, when they did eat, they said *"Bismillah"* with each bite. They never touched food without ablution. In this way, they ensured that whatever sustenance entered their bodies was light. And with that light, they flew. We see this care reflected in the personal examples of our present shaykhs, as those who lived in previous times saw these traits in the earlier true shaykhs.

Knowing this, we can choose how rigorously we apply *halal* rules to our own diet, but we must realize that this will affect our progress. If we find ourselves unable to advance, we must not repeat the same self-destructive acts over and over like crazy people. Rather we must seek out the source of our problem and correct it. If we wish to receive the most precious treasures, we must be disciplined.

THE IMPORTANCE OF EXERCISE

The human body requires food and drink. However, not everything that we consider food and drink is digestible or useful to the human body. Rather than providing fuel for the body, precipitates of these unconverted nutrients may settle as sediment. Since the body cannot dispose of them naturally, they may accumulate over time, and that can cause various illnesses.

Initially, such sediments may manifest as localized accumulations before they affect the blood and are transported through the blood stream

THE HEALING POWER OF SUFI MEDITATION

to the rest of the body. In these cases, the condition may first manifest itself in the form of bowel problems. With time, this buildup of sediment may become more dangerous, manifesting as localized illnesses that may spread in the body. It is therefore important to study the pathology of a sickness or disease, and the history of its development.

Often, immediate and extreme "cures" are administered, with no care given to the history of a disease's spread. Strong purgatives are sometimes administered. This not only fails to cure the underlying ailment, but may also exacerbate the problem or create new ones. Indeed, most drugs in this category are toxic. At best, they force the body to eliminate the good with the bad. They are, in the terminology of some traditional medical knowledge, "hot." They may therefore weaken the immune system, predispose patients to arrhythmias, impact kidney function, and lead to the development of various other disorders and deficiencies.

A more appropriate treatment for such disorders is exercise. Appropriate physical exercise is necessary to refresh the organs, ease the flow of food and nutrients, enhance digestion, and prevent such accumulations. Furthermore, natural and methodical control of muscular action lightens the spirit, refreshes the mind, rejuvenates the organs, strengthens muscular tone, prevents callousness of the joints, strengthens the tendons and ligaments, lessens the possibility of somatic disorders, abates most illnesses, and improves the overall well-being of the self.

Of course, care must be taken concerning the level of physical exercises, with particular attention given to issues of balance, moderation, and intensity. In general, routines dedicated to any particular limb strengthen it, just as dedicating one's thoughts to a specific subject strengthens one's memory. Hence, each part of the body requires specific routines.

The lungs, for example, require reading exercise, beginning with silent reading and progressing gradually in intensity and loudness. Hearing exercises require careful responsive attention, thereby stimulating the auditory nerves and ears. Speaking exercises increase oral command. Optical exercises strengthen both physical and mental vision. It is even possible, by following a careful regimen, to strengthen the ocular muscles and correct both nearsightedness and farsightedness.

Sports can provide an enjoyable means of exercise. Hiking, swimming, walking at a moderate pace, horseback riding, archery, and similar sports are the most healthful for the entire body. Adopting such programs of physical exercise can even cure chronic illnesses such as anemia, infectious diseases, ulcers, and colic, among others.

Understanding the Secrets of Iron

Iron is the most important element in the body. It is what allows each of us to generate his own electromagnetic field. Iron also acts as a receptor, which is why it is so important to maintain its purity. If the iron that is within our bodies is pure, it can function as a powerful antenna, allowing each of our cells to become a receiver for Divine Energy during Sufi meditation.

Understanding the secrets of iron is a key to spiritual development, particularly at this time. In this world, iron has long been the bedrock of technology and industry. It was the development of iron-working that allowed previously insignificant civilizations like the Hittites to triumph over Bronze Age cultures like those of the Babylonians and Egyptians. The study of iron led to the discovery of magnetism, which helped usher in the Age of Exploration and gave rise to a new global trading order that would ultimately bring both hemispheres of the world together. Iron was an essential ingredient in the Industrial Revolution that gave birth to the modern world as we know it. And iron has continued to be important, playing a central role in the development of early computer technology. Indeed, it is still to be found everywhere—even within us.

Time and time again throughout human history, it was the physical mastery of iron that allowed one people to exert its will over another.

Iron, therefore, has long been a universal symbol of power and might. Nevertheless, the full potential of iron has rarely been understood, for its true power lies not in its physical properties, but rather in its spiritual properties.

Islamic history is rich in examples of the material power of iron, and these provide a clear indication of the importance with which this metal was viewed. Consider, for example, what God says about the Prophet David ﷺ. Being a prophetic king, Prophet David ﷺ represented the merging of temporal and spiritual power, the application of spiritual authority to mundane reality; in this, Prophet David ﷺ was like the Prophet and king Solomon ﷺ. Regarding him, the Holy Quran states:

> We bestowed grace aforetime on David from Ourselves.
> O ye mountains! Sing ye back the praises of God with
> him, and ye birds as well! And We made the iron soft
> for him. (34:10)

Sayyidina Zhul-Qarnain, another king, used the power of iron to imprison chaos and evil, embodied by Gog and Magog, as described by the Holy Quran:

> They said, "O Zhul-Qarnain! The Gog and Magog
> do great mischief on earth; shall we then render you
> tribute in order that you might erect a barrier between
> us and them?"

> He said, "(The power) in which my Lord has estab-
> lished me is better (than tribute); help me therefore
> with strength and (labor): I will erect a strong barrier
> between you and them:

> "Bring me blocks of iron." At length, when he had
> filled up the space between the two steep mountain-
> sides, he said, "Blow (with your bellows)!" Then, when
> he had made it (red) as fire, he said, "Bring me, that I
> may pour over it, molten lead.

*Thus they were made powerless to scale it or to dig
through it.*

He said, "This is a mercy from my Lord ... (18:94-98)

Another clue to the importance of iron lies in the fact that iron is
not produced on Earth. Rather, all the iron that exists on Earth came
from the cosmos, where it was produced in the fiery atomic furnaces of
the stars. Scientists have only recently come to realize this important
fact, but the Holy Quran made it quite clear more than 1,400 years
ago:

*And We sent down iron, wherein is mighty power, as
well as many benefits for mankind. (57:25)*

Islam also provides the keys to unlocking the spiritual secrets of
iron. Surah 57 of the Holy Quran is entitled *Al-Hadid,* or "Iron."
Correspondingly, the fifty-seventh name of Prophet ﷺ is *al-Mahdi,*
signifying the particular relevance of iron to the Last Days. Al-Mahdi
is the Guide, teaching us that iron is essential for guidance on both the
physical and spiritual planes. This correspondence also has important
implications for those who are seeking to be of service to *Sayyidina*
Mahdi ﷺ.

The Arabic word for iron, *hadid,* is spelled with the letters *Hah,
dal, ya, dal,* and is comprised of two root words: *had* and *yad. Had*
means "blade." *Yad* means "hand." Thus, the root of the Arabic word
for iron translates to "blade hand." This signifies the importance of iron
with regards to spiritual and physical power, and its relevance as an
instrument to manifest the Will of God.

The significance of iron is elaborated in an important Tradition of
the Prophet ﷺ:

God's Messenger ﷺ said, "When God created the Earth it
began to oscillate, so He created the mountains, ordered them
onto it, and it became steady. The angels marveled at the
strength of the mountains and asked their Lord whether there

was anything in His creation stronger than the mountains, to which he replied that iron was stronger. They asked if anything in His creation was stronger than iron, and He replied that fire was. They asked if anything in His creation was stronger than fire, and He replied that water was. They asked if anything in His creation was stronger than water, and He replied that wind was."

The deeply spiritual underlying meaning of this Tradition outlines the stages of personal progress and spiritual achievement. The mountains refer to the saints of God, who—through great firmness of faith—reach a station that allows them to balance the universe with positive energy and divine light. Like the mountains, they are unshakeable in their faith, solid and stable in their devotion and service to God Almighty [1]. Through continuing practice and devotion, the saint may become like iron: absolutely firm and unbreakable. The next station is that of fire, wherein the saint's essence burns with love for its Creator and is ignited by the flames of Divine Energy from the Presence of God. Before this fiery radiance, even iron melts, just as the soul of the saint is annihilated in the Divine Presence. The saint thereby becomes an empty vessel containing the water of complete submission, a fluid essence that responds automatically and instantaneously to the Divine Will. This is the Station of Annihilation in the Ocean of Power, within which swims all of creation. Finally, the saint may advance to the station of the wind, the pure Prophetic Essence—a level of being without mass, subtle and ethereal, the pure representation of the Divine Will.

The common individual is far from these realities and is instead weak, vulnerable, and easily broken. Such is the result of asserting one's

---

[1] at-Tirmidhi, Chapter 119:3578.

personal will. However, if one submits to the guidance of a master and begins a spiritual practice, one may use Sufi meditation to reach these states and tap their realities.

IRON AND MAGNETISM

All of creation maintains its essential order through the power of magnetism and electromagnetic fields. As alluded to earlier, iron is an essential element in magnetism. Thus, if we wish to control ourselves, we must learn to control our magnetic field. To control our magnetic fields, we must learn to control the iron that is within us.

To understand this process, consider the following example from modern science. If you take a wire, attach it to an iron rod, and connect the other end of that wire to a battery, nothing will happen. However, if you wrap that same wire around the iron rod a hundred times and then connect it to the battery, you will have created a magnet. Moreover, once you take the coil of wire from that iron rod, the rod will retain some of that magnetic quality—it will remain a magnet, although somewhat weaker than it was with the current coiling around it.

Each of us is like that iron rod. We are all made up of protons, neutrons, and electrons. But our potential is latent. For most of us, it remains untapped. However, when we coil ourselves in the spiritual dress of the Shaykh and then connect our hearts to his heart, we too become magnetized. The energy we receive from him electrifies us and unleashes our hidden potential. This is because the Shaykh's light with which we dress ourselves is composed of many layers. Each layer—each coil, so to speak—represents the mantle of a different Shaykh of this Order, continuing back from master to master all the way back to the Master of Masters, *Sayyidina* Muhammad ﷺ.

This is the secret of the Reality of Attraction, one of the six powers conferred upon and realized by the Naqshbandi follower when he totally and completely surrenders his will to that of the Shaykh.

Spiritual attraction, like physical magnetism, is founded in the secret of the light of the Prophet ﷺ, for it is his Holy Light that is the essence of the unity of creation. That pure Light is cloaked by the density of this world, by the veils that separate us from reality—this density and these veils imprison us on this material plane and imprison our souls in our bodies. Saints are those who have penetrated this curtain and ripped aside the illusory veils of this world by abandoning it and devoting themselves instead to the practices of asceticism. They have not been deceived by the imaginary freedoms that are held in such high esteem by the lovers of this world. Instead, they have denied the demands of their bodies and the whining whims of their egos. As a result of their sincere efforts and longing for their Creator, they shine brightly with the Light of the Prophet ﷺ.

The Light of the Prophet ﷺ is that pure essence which is based in unity and which is, therefore, naturally attractive to all that has become separated from the primordial state of unity. It is because of this that a person in the presence of a saint who completely manifests the Light of the Prophet ﷺ feels powerfully attracted to him. That is because the soul is seeking to restore its lost union, to reunite itself with the ocean from which it came. When it feels the presence of that sublime sea, it longs to plunge into it, to lose itself in that primordial essence.

That is why the practice of Sufi meditation is so important for the sincere seeker of truth and reality. In Sufi meditation he seeks to annihilate himself in the presence of the master; then, through him, in the presence of the Prophet ﷺ; then, though him, in the Divine Presence itself. Being dressed with the light of the master then becomes analogous to being an iron rod with a copper wire wound around it. Each time we practice Sufi meditation, we wrap that wire around the rod another time until there are hundreds and then thousands of coils. Ultimately, by maintaining perpetual presence with the master, that rod is coiled beyond any counting. It awaits only the permission of the master, which is analogous to connecting that wire to a battery, to unleash the tremendous power that is then latent within it. The sincere and humble follower then becomes a powerful magnet, drawing lost souls towards their own realities and unity.

Iron is particularly relevant to this process, because it is the iron within our systems that binds this energy, this spiritual light, inside us. That is why it is vitally important that the iron within one's system be purified and perfected, for the state of the iron inside our bodies directly impacts the quality of the electromagnetic energy field, or aura, that surrounds us.

The process of purifying the iron that is within us is both spiritual and physical. So, too, is the process of maintaining that purity.

On the spiritual level, this purification is accomplished through the practice of Sufi meditation. That is why one who has developed a strong spiritual connection with the master, and through him with the Prophet 卌, will exhibit a brilliant and attractive aura, a fact that will be clearly visible to those who have developed the form of seeing necessary to perceive that which is beyond the visual spectrum.

However, this is only part of the purification process. To fully cleanse and purify the blood requires physical, as well as spiritual, action.

PURIFYING THE BLOOD

Most of the body's iron is stored in the blood, which is also the mechanism by which this essential element is conveyed throughout the body. Therefore, to purify the iron that is within the body, it is necessary to purify the blood.

Women have a natural cycle that cleanses the "bad iron" from their blood each month. Men are not so fortunate. They have no natural means of eliminating the negatively charged iron that builds up within their blood. That is why, by the age of 40, a man will typically have twice as much iron in his blood as a woman. It is, therefore, hardly surprising that men suffer twice the rate of cancer, diabetes and heart disease. Men are also more prone to infection, because bacteria, viruses, and fungi all utilize iron as a primary growth factor. In essence, the lower iron level in females gives them a measure of protection from these pathogens.

For men, the means of releasing negatively charged iron is bloodletting, traditionally administered through the Islamic practice of cupping. This fact was revealed by the Prophet ﷺ himself, and it was practiced by the Companions ‾ and later generations of Muslims. Cupping has its own prophetic methodology and both inner and outer dimensions.

For some, the practice of bloodletting has negative connotations. They associate it with backwards medical practices. In fact, bloodletting is enjoying a tremendous resurgence as modern medical professionals come to understand the logic and biological principles behind it. Today, conventional physicians have begun experimenting with bloodletting as a means of treating Alzheimer's disease, Parkinson's disease, cancer, diabetes, and other chronic ailments. Recent studies have also shown that those who give blood regularly are healthier than those who do not.

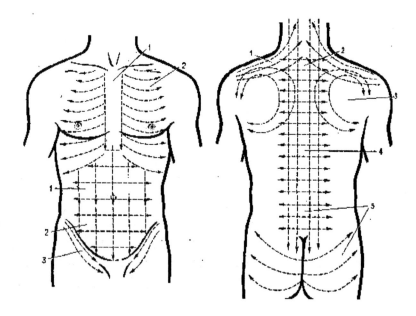

Acting upon the advice of Prophet Muhammad ﷺ, the Companions underwent this important treatment twice a year. In men, iron carrying impurities is deposited in the back, at the shoulders and at the base of the spine, or coccyx. It was here that the bad blood was removed. In practicing cupping today, it is important to pay attention to these details, as well as proper hygiene and sanitary practices.

SECTION THREE: HEALING WITH DIVINE ENERGY

Spiritual healing is not at all a mysterious process, but is in fact quite straightforward, though the techniques employed may be very complex. Spiritual healing taps the energy field that exists around each of us. As we have seen, everyone has an electromagnetic energy field, or aura, that surrounds and interpenetrates his or her physical body. This field is intimately associated with the health of the human being. The most effective way of treating health anomalies is by working on this field directly. In spiritual healing, Divine Energy is used to manipulate these energy patterns within and around the human body.

The force of a waterfall can be harnessed to produce electricity and light. This is analogous to the manner in which Divine Energy is used in spiritual healing. The energy that flows in our bodies—if channeled through a properly balanced system that is in equilibrium —can be harnessed to battle disease, strengthen weak organs, and maintain good health. Improving the flow of Divine Energy through the body brings vitality and makes the body better able to maintain its own health. Moreover, spiritual healing allows the Divine Energy within the body to be exponentially expanded and focused in order to heal afflictions in areas where there is pain, disease, or other disorders. Once the healing process has begun, the energy latent within the body can increasingly be used to restore overall equilibrium and good health.

A similar phenomenon is seen in an atomic reaction, where tremendous power is released by converting a small amount of physical mass into a great amount of energy in accordance with the formula $E=MC^2$. The energy produced increases exponentially as the activated, energized atom spreads its energy to its neighbors, propagating a chain reaction of energy release. Spiritual healers use this same principle to harness Divine Energy and activate the life force within the patient. They also channel Divine Energy to those areas that need healing power.

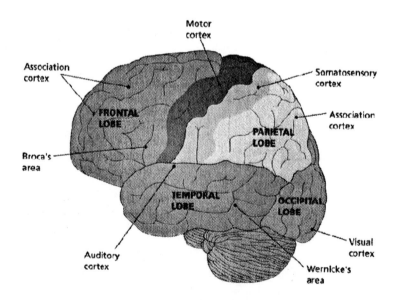

THE THREE PHASES OF SPIRITUAL HEALING

In spiritual healing, Divine Energy is first channeled to the cerebral cortex, which is the seat of thought within the human brain. From there, the energy is intensely focused and channeled in the nuclei of the brain stem cells, which are activated and stimulated by this focused life force. As a result, impulses are sent to the autonomic nervous system, which regulates bodily functions, restoring the body to equilibrium and causing it to release pain-blocking peptides into the brain. This concentration of energy in the brain represents the first phase of spiritual healing.

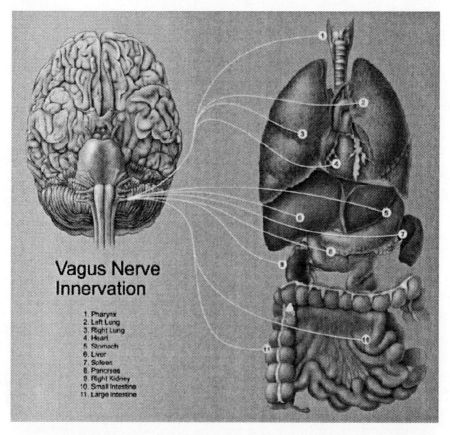

Vagus Nerve Innervation

1. Pharynx
2. Left Lung
3. Right Lung
4. Heart
5. Stomach
6. Liver
7. Spleen
8. Pancreas
9. Right Kidney
10. Small Intestine
11. Large Intestine

This process in turn stimulates the vagus nerve, which sends electrical impulses to the heart's conduction system, the sinoatrial node, through the internodal tracts, to the atrioventricular node, down the bundle of His, out the Purkinje fibers and into the myocardial wall to begin systole.

This migration of energy, which fills the heart, is the second phase of spiritual healing.

❖ Conditions such as angina,

❖ congestive heart failure,

❖ cardiomyopathy, and

❖ hypertension, in addition to many other related cardiac diseases, can be healed through this process.

In the third and final stage of healing, the Divine Energy is pumped with the blood out of the heart into the vascular system and delivered throughout the entire body. A major focus of phase three is the aorta, which is the conduit for the healing waves of energy that are carried by the blood. As the blood flows from the heart, it is first channeled back to the heart via the coronary arteries in a chain reaction that sustains and increases the energy in the heart itself, in much the same way that the sun increases its light through its own nuclear reactions. This cycle produces more and more energy, which pours out into the vascular system with foci in the major arteries, supplying the brain via the carotid arteries. It also travels through the subclavian arteries to the upper extremities, through splanchnic circulation to the abdomen, through the renal arteries to the kidneys, and through the iliac vessels to the lower extremities. Through this process, the healing energy is carried to every cell of the body. Just as a river feeds the plant and animal life that lives along its banks, so too does this flow nourish and revive all the cells that draw from it.

A healthy heart will sustain a weak body, but when the heart is weak and diseased—even in a young person—the body will not be healthy or live long. Therefore, maintaining the heart is the first priority for spiritual healers. Maintaining the brain and nervous system is another important priority, as these regulate the rest of the body's functions.

HIGH SENSE PERCEPTION AS A DIAGNOSTIC TOOL

Modern physicians use magnetic resonance imaging (MRI) to obtain images of the internal conditions of the human body, and to detect any diseases or disorders that may be present. Such technology uses energy and the alignment of the body's atoms to create images. It should come as no surprise that spiritual healers are able to use similar forces as their own diagnostic tools, the most important of which is what is now commonly referred to in scientific circles as high sense perception, or HSP.

Simply put, HSP is a means of perceiving things beyond the normal range of the five senses. In other words, it refers to the ability to see, hear, smell, taste, and touch things that cannot normally be perceived. HSP includes those abilities that have been referred to variously as clairvoyance, clairaudience, remote sensing, and extra-sensory perception, or ESP. It is not imagination, but an authentic perception of reality.

HSP reveals the dynamic world of interacting fields of Divine Energy that surround and permeate all living things. This energy supports us, nourishes us, and gives us life. We can also use this energy to sense each other, because we are all connected by it. So, too, is the world around us, as well as the unseen world of realities that is behind the veil of this world. That means that the same techniques can be used to obtain real sensory data from these as well.

In spiritual healing, HSP can be used to discern the pathophysiology of pain and disease. Indeed, for the experienced healer, such aberrations on the energy level appear right before their eyes, so to speak. HSP reveals how most diseases are initiated in the energy field.

Distortions in the energy field caused over time by unhealthy living habits are transmitted to the body, manifesting as serious illness. The source or initiating cause of this process may be psychological trauma, physical trauma, or a combination of both. Understanding how a disease or disorder was initiated allows the healer to determine how to reverse the process, repair the damage, and heal the ailment. Thus, the ability to perceive spiritual energies and auras aids healers in formulating their diagnosis and determining the best course of treatment. Learning how to use HSP is, therefore, an essential part of the spiritual healer's training.

To develop HSP, it is necessary to enter into an expanded state of consciousness. There are many means to achieve this, but Sufi meditation is by far the best.

The Nasma and Meditation

In the terminology of Sufi spirituality, the non-physical body is called the *nasma*. The *nasma* exists within each physical body as a subtle manifestation of Divine Energy. The *nasma* is present in human beings just as rose water is present in the rose or as fire is present in glowing coals. Because of its connection to the Divine Energy source, it can taste without using the tongue, can see without using the eyes, and can hear without using the ears.

By using their *nasma*, healers are able to tap the powers of HSP. The *nasma* derives its nourishment from the Divine Energy that is released whenever we act, think, or form a belief or intention. The *nasma* in human beings is capable of leaving the physical body at any time through its connection with the universal driving force.

When the flow of Divine Energy is disturbed or impaired, the health of the patient is adversely affected, leading to pain, disease, distress, and so forth. These are signals that we need to rebalance our energy. A positive energy flow nourishes the *nasma* and maintains its structure and foundation, balancing the human system. This balance leads to increased awareness of the body's sensations, which leads to good living, proper diet, and enjoyment of exercise. The *nasma* then supports and maintains a healthy physical body in which the chemical and physical systems remain balanced and functioning normally—all of this sustains good physical health.

The energies in a healthy body remain balanced but on top of that they also support and positively influence the energy balance in other peoples' bodies. The *nasma* can influence others like a magnet, bringing the charges of adjacent metal into its alignment. Therefore, the energy of a healthy system not only heals the self, but also promotes better health and spiritual harmony in those around the healthy person. Good health and a healthy aura may then be seen as self-propagating, for their effects extend to those people who come into contact with the healthy person.

The relationship between the *nasma* and the physical body is, however, a two-way street. Just as correcting problems in the *nasma* can restore health to the physical body, problems with the physical body—particularly those that affect the organs—can weaken and disrupt it.

For example, a weak body can lead to a weakened *nasma*, and this can affect the patient both mentally and physically. In the mental sphere, this can manifest itself as neurosis, depression, hysteria, psychosis, seizures, sleep terror, and insomnia. If left untreated, the *nasma* may become so weak that it is rendered incapable of defending itself within the weakened body. As a result, the patient may suffer seizures, psychotic fits, or display irrationally aggressive behavior. However, a spiritual healer can strengthen the patient's organs and thereby strengthen the *nasma* through the power of Divine Energy, creating a heightened energy state within the patient that eliminates the symptoms of the sickness and restores proper balance to the system.

MEDITATION AND THE FOCAL POINT OF TREATMENT

In the philosophy of spiritual healing, good physical health is inseparable from mental and spiritual well-being. Therefore, the maintenance of good health requires intense and continuous striving by the patient for personal change and improvement. The development of patience, contentment, gratitude, cheerfulness, joy, love, sharing, courage, benefaction, recognition of good deeds, forbearance, and courtesy improves spiritual harmony and strengthens the flow of Divine Energy within the body. Spiritual health requires the practice of spirituality.

One of the most effective means of promoting spiritual health is meditation, (*muraqabah*). The meditative exercises described in the first chapter of this book promote the development of good characteristics, and also open a channel between the individual and what is called in some traditions the "higher self"—that spark of divinity that connects each of us to the Divine Presence.

By communicating with this "higher self," we may gain valuable insights into the underlying factors behind any health problems we may be experiencing. We may also receive advice on how best to treat or correct these disorders. Those trained in the healing arts may even be able to learn what specific treatments to apply to heal themselves or others.

On a more basic level, meditation has been proven an effective therapeutic technique that promotes deep relaxation and mental quiet. This reduces the overall stress level of the body and mind, promoting chemical and hormonal equilibrium throughout the body. Indeed, medical tests have shown that there are definite, measurable physiological changes in meditating subjects. The brain itself undergoes changes in the type of electrical waves generated. Electroencephalogram (EEG) results show that meditation increases the generation of alpha waves, and in some subjects, increases theta wave activity. These indicate a shift of consciousness into a tranquil state of awareness quite different from that of sleep. This state is therapeutic and very restful, although the patient remains fully conscious and functional.

According to recent research, the body responds to meditation in a variety of other ways as well. The breathing pattern and heart rate slow, and there is a decrease in the level of oxygen consumption and carbon dioxide elimination. Further, the beneficial physical effects of meditation last beyond the meditation period. For instance, sufferers of hypertension and many other diseases have, through meditation alone, made such clinically measurable improvements that they have been able to discontinue their medications.

How Energy Relates to Disease

Spiritual healers symbolize the flow of Divine Energy within the body as vortices made up of a number of smaller spirals of energy. These are known in Sufi terminology as *lata'if* (singular: *lateefa*), meaning subtle manifestations or layers. These are the Nine Points of the Self. They are also related to the *chakras* of Kundalini Yoga, which is a central part of both Hindu and Buddhist mysticism, and to the nodes of the Tree of Life, a key concept in Jewish Kabalistic spirituality.

These nodes are the points of maximum energy intake and are very important focal points of balance within the body's energy system. Disease and illness occur if one or more of these points are unbalanced. In adults, *lata'if* have a protective screen over them. In a healthy system, each *lata'if* spins in synchronicity with the others, drawing power from the universal field of Divine Energy into their centers for use by the body. Each one of them is attuned to a specific frequency, and maintaining this tuning is vital to bodily health.

In a diseased system, these vortices are not synchronized. The energy of the *lata'if* may cycle too quickly, too slowly, or perhaps erratically, irregularly, or in an imbalanced way. In the most serious cases, breaks in the entire energy pattern can be observed. These disruptions may be caused by a *lateefa* that is fully or partially collapsed or inverted. These disturbances are related to dysfunction or pathology of the physical body in that area.

HEALING THROUGH MEDITATION AND FOCAL POINTS OF THE LATA'IF

As mentioned earlier, there are nine *lata'if*. Seven of these are particularly important in spiritual healing. Two of these are located above and below the heart, two above and below the left breast, two above and below the right breast, and one on the forehead. Each of these vortices is associated with a different color of energy, and each of these energies has different effects on specific illnesses.

The two centers above and below the heart are green. The two centers above and below the left breast are yellow. The two centers above and below the right breast are black. The center of the forehead is white.

By meditating on these points, the seeker can activate them and generate energy. When each of these *lata'if* is stimulated, it attracts Divine Energy of the same frequency from the universal field of cosmic energy. To activate these nodes, visualize them as tiny floating spheres of heavenly light. The size of these spheres depends on which *lateefa* is activated, as there is a different sized sphere for each of the different colors.

In treating illness, the healer activates the appropriate *lateefa* needed to cure that particular sickness or disorder. In turn, the *lateefa* produces more of its energy color, which then attracts more energy of the same frequency from the universal source of Divine Energy. This creates a positive feedback loop that transforms the activated vortex into a shimmering globe of heavenly light, through which pours Divine Energy. This Divine Energy builds up within the healer to the point that he or she emits light and heat. When fully energized, the healer channels this Divine Energy to the patient by massaging the affected areas of the body. As the healer massages the locus of the ailment, Divine Energy in the form of heat is transferred from the hands, while Divine Energy in the form of light is transferred from the forehead to the patient. This light cannot be seen physically, but it is readily apparent to those with developed spiritual sight.

After thus beginning the healing process, the healer will prescribe specific recitations (*dhikr*) to be performed by the patient while sitting alone in a fully relaxed state. These daily devotions will complete the cure.

In general, the prescribed recitations will be one or more of God's Divine Names and Attributes. These Holy Names are like sparks of Divine Energy. Each time they are mentioned, they draw more and more Divine Energy into the body of the patient. This further stimulates the vortices of the *lata'if*, which in turn generate even more healing energy within the body. Though this energy is less intense than that administered by the healer, it is nonetheless sufficient to cause the patient to break out in a sweat. When that occurs, the patient returns to the healer for another energy treatment.

The healer proceeds as before, further advancing the patient's recovery. As the moon reflects the light of the sun onto the Earth, so too does the healer reflect Divine Energy from its universal source through his or her body and into the body of the patient. This spiritual interaction between the healer and the patient may be repeated for several days or even weeks until the patient fully recovers.

During the recovery process, the patient begins to experience a positive psychological effect from the dynamic, synergistic interaction with the healer. This further speeds recovery and relief from pain by inducing the endocrine glands to secrete hormones that balance the body's systems and begin to cure malfunctioning or damaged organs. As a result, the patient's mental and spiritual health improve along with his physical health.

Section Four: Secrets of Ablution and the Powers of the Hands

Our Prophet ﷺ explained very well what God has set for us as right and wrong. The Prophet ﷺ was the first to explain it, and God said of him:

> *We have not sent you except as a Mercy to the worlds.*
> (21:107)

Whatever benefits us, the Prophet ﷺ was responsible to deliver the information regarding it to us. If he did not deliver this information, he would be asked why not. God entrusted him with complete knowledge of what He had created, and this knowledge was revealed through the

Prophet's ﷺ Message. Through that Message, the Prophet ﷺ was able to reach every person during and after his time.

Part of that Message dealt with power and energy. The Prophet ﷺ taught his Companions about the use of human and divine energy, and about the different powers that exist around us in this world. Moreover, he showed his Companions how to use these powers to heal.

Prophetic healing is one of the central sciences of Islam. The Prophet ﷺ taught a variety of methods for curing and healing. The essence of this science can be found in the Tradition of the blind man who came to Prophet ﷺ and asked him to restore his sight.

The Prophet ﷺ said:

Go make ablution, perform two cycles of prayer, and then say: "Oh Allah, I ask You and turn to You through my Prophet Muhammad, the Prophet of mercy; Ya Muhammad, I seek your intercession with my Lord for the return of my eyesight."

The Prophet ﷺ also added that this prayer can be used for any need, saying, "And if there is some need, do the same."[1]

The Prophet ﷺ taught the blind man the prayer, but he did not say to him, "Go and read the prayer I have given you." Rather, the Prophet ﷺ first instructed the man to make ablution, thus making it clear that performing ablution is the first step in healing. This advice was not only for the blind man. Rather, it is a general principle of prophetic healing. It demonstrates that the first step in curing any illness is ablution. Without ablution, our healing abilities are vastly weakened.

THE PRINCIPLES OF ABLUTION

Ablution increases the energy available to us, allowing us to tap into a power that is thousands of times greater than what we would be able to access otherwise. This is why the Prophet ﷺ told the blind man to first make ablution.

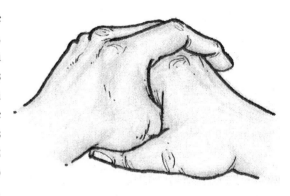

Of course, for our ablution to be effective, it must be made with full attention to its exoteric and esoteric details.

Healing begins with ablution, and ablution begins with intention. After intention, the next step is to wash your hands up to the wrists. The first movement of ablution is centered upon the hands. Here, too, is another sign for us. It signifies that the first level of energy is in the hands.

In telling the blind man to make ablution, which begins with the hands, the Prophet ﷺ hinted that the man could heal himself using that energy. Therefore we see that more than 1,400 years ago, the Prophet ﷺ was teaching how to heal with energy. Another meaning of this instruction to make ablution is that the first step in the healing process is to purify oneself using ablution. For this reason, the Prophet ﷺ said that ablution is the armor of the believer, granting him protection from the enemy.

When we make ablution, we begin with our hands. We rub them, turning the right over the left and the left over the right. This order is very important. The seeker cannot begin with the left over the right. He must begin with the right over the left. Then he cleans between the fingers, intertwining them with the right thumb on the left and the left thumb on the right and so on.

Reading the Divine Code

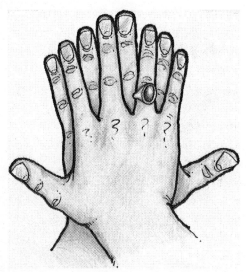

Let us consider what is symbolized in this procedure. First, we are using ten fingers. Ten is a number composed of two digits, one and zero. These two digits, zero and one, form the basis of the binary code, the language of computers. They are keys to unlocking the power of computers. God taught this code to the first programmers without their knowledge, allowing mankind to tap into this power with machines. This energy is now being channeled through computers, and we are witnessing a myriad of miraculous wonders as a result of this power in the world today. Of course, the programmers that are using this divine code to tap into this power are using it without knowing why it works. They do not understand the Islamic aspect—the divine aspect—of this knowledge.

We can begin to understand the divine significance of one and zero if we look at our hands. If you open your hand and draw a line connecting each of the fingertips, it will form a circle. This circle is approximately twenty centimeters in diameter. Similarly, one can draw a circle around the extended human body, much as Leonardo da Vinci did in his famous sketch. Therefore, the whole body can be represented in the hand.

This is the central teaching of reflexology, which uses different points on the hand to heal different parts of the body. A practitioner of reflexology will apply pressure or heat to these points in order to effect a cure. But the highest level is to stimulate these points without touching them.

In Islamic healing, the hand can act as a receiver of positive energy. Advanced students of this art are able to see the circle formed by their bodies, to see it as a sort of parabolic dish, one that collects and focuses the Divine Energy of the cosmos through their bodies and into their hearts. They do not think this. They do not imagine this. They *see* this.

As we have said, the circle of the body is reflected on a smaller scale in the circle of the hand. This same energy can be drawn in through the hands and channeled throughout the body. That is why we begin with the hands.

When we rub the hands during ablution, we activate this energy— the power of one and zero. We activate the code that God has given us through the hands. That is why it is important to begin by rubbing with the right hand over the left and then the left over the right.

If we stand in front of a mirror, we see that our right is left and our left is right – in the mirror they are the opposite of what we normally consider them to be. That is a metaphor for the fact that this world, and our presence in it, is not reality. Rather, it is an *image* of reality. In the heavenly realm, which is the true reality, left is right and right is left.

That is why everything that is done here, in this world, is done counterclockwise, not clockwise. Here, for example, during Hajj, we perform the circumambulation of the Ka'ba counterclockwise. In the afterlife, circumambulation of the Throne is clockwise. That is why the left hand has to submit to the right, and the right hand has to submit to the left.

When you rub your hands together in this way, you activate the power of the 99 Beautiful Names and Attributes that God has inscribed upon your hands. The effect is not unlike what occurs when one rubs two sticks together. The friction between the two pieces of wood creates energy, in this case in the form of heat, ultimately releasing itself in the form of fire.

Likewise, rubbing your hands together creates energy, and rubbing them together under water locks in that energy, preventing it from escaping. The water keeps this energy in the body, whence it can be released later.

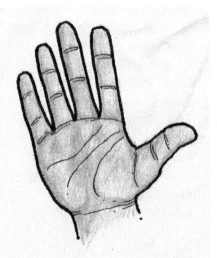

However, when we want to heal someone, we want that energy to be released immediately. Therefore, we do not use water. Instead, we rub the hands together in the same manner, then open them to release the energy that has been generated. The energy that is released is different from the energy that has been collected, because it has been processed using the heavenly code that is hidden within the hands.

If you look at your right hand, you will see that the number 18 {in Arabic |^} is imprinted upon it. If you study your left hand, you will see that the number 81 is inscribed there. If you add those two numbers together, their sum is 99, the number of Divine Names/Attributes of God. Moreover, both 18 and 81 are comprised of the numerals 1 and

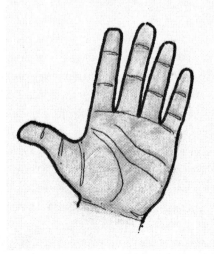

8. If those two numerals are added together, their sum is 9 (1 + 8 = 9; 8 + 1 = 9), so again we see the number 99 reflected in the two hands (9 on one and 9 on the other). And 99 itself reduces down, in numerology, to the number 9 (9 + 9 = 18 = 1 + 8 = 9); this number is also signified by each of the hands.

The number 9 is significant in Islamic healing because it refers to the Nine Points of the Self. These nine points represent the nine saints that are responsible for the self. Furthermore, they are the same nine points that form the Enneagram— a symbolic methodology employed by Western psychologists that, in fact, was originally taught by the Naqshbandi masters of Central Asia.

When you rub the fingers together, you activate the 99 Beautiful Names and Attributes of God. You also activate the Nine Points of the body. And, when you activate them, they begin to function like a receiver. This receiver is capable of drawing in Divine Energy and focusing it, just as today's satellite television dishes draw in digital signals from orbiting spacecraft, process them, and display them as pictures and sounds.

As explained above, the hands also form circles and are capable of functioning in a similar fashion. That is why, when we rub our hands together, the energy we thereby generate is concentrated so strongly. The emanations of Divine Energy received by the hands are processed through the filter of the Divine Names and Attributes inscribed upon them and represented by them—just as algorithmic codes are used by computers to process digital signals, unscrambling that transmitted energy and forming it into logical patterns that can stimulate various responses and functions in the equipment they are fed into. The codes contained in the hands are even more complex, for there are even more secrets hidden within these numbers.

As demonstrated above, the hands are coded to represent the numerals 8 and 1 and 1 and 8. We have seen how both sets of numbers can be combined to form the number 9. In Islamic numerology, 9 equals 0—it is the number of submission which cannot be multiplied without creating a number that can be reduced to 9 (for example: $9 \times 2 = 18 \rightarrow 1 + 8 = 9$; $9 \times 3 = 27 \rightarrow 2 + 7 = 9$; $4 \times 9 = 36 \rightarrow 3 + 6 = 9$, etc.), just as zero multiplied by any number <u>must</u> produce zero.

On an esoteric level, this number represents complete submission. Therefore, when we activate this code on the level of Divine Energy, we submit to that heavenly power. Using the special properties coded within the number 9, we effectively negate ourselves, becoming instead channels for that Divine Energy. Like lightning rods in a storm, the divine emanations that surround us are channeled through us, concentrated, and released.

Such is the power of these heavenly codes, and even this is only the beginning of the secrets contained in these divine numbers. But there are still other numbers coded in our hands. The number 19 is one of them, and it can be activated through ablution.

As the hands represent the number 9, each of the fingers represents the number 1. The fingers of each hand combine to form the number 5 and, when the fingers are interlaced during ablution these combine to form the number 10, which—added to the 9 signified by each hand—activates the power of the number 19. Do not omit this part of ablution because this is part of its perfection, in it is the key to unlocking the code of 19.

The number 19 is particularly significant, for it is the number upon which the Holy Quran is based. Every verse of the Quran is founded upon the number 19. 19 is the number of the angels that will hold Hellfire on the Day of Judgment.

THE ENERGY OF HELLFIRE

Hellfire is energy: powerful, negative energy. But though that energy is negatively charged, it is not necessarily bad. This negative energy can be used to heal. Again, God has provided examples for us in modern medical science.

Today, doctors treat bacterial infections by administering poisons to the body. These poisons are specially focused to target the bacteria, killing the microscopic invaders and thereby restoring the patient to good health. These poisons are called antibiotics. Chemotherapy is the use of poisonous chemicals to kill cancer cells. They may even use radiation, which is normally toxic to the human body, to treat those afflicted by that disease.

Thus, we should not be surprised to learn that negative energy can also be used for healing purposes, particularly when we consider another important mathematical principle: multiplying two negative numbers always produces a positive number. Therefore, when one negative energy is directed at another, both are transformed into positively charged energy. This is how healers can tap into the negative energy of Hellfire and use it for positive, therapeutic purposes. Thus applied, that negative energy attacks the poisons that are within the patient's system and changes them into positively charged forces that then begin to heal.

COMPLETING THE HEALING PROCESS

The numerals eight and one also have angelic significance, as is mentioned in the Holy Quran:

> *And the angels will be on its sides, and eight will,*
> *that Day, bear the Throne of your Lord above them.*
> (69:17)

When God's Throne comes on Judgment Day, there will be eight angels carrying it. The eight will be carrying the One. So here, too, we see the numbers 8 and 1—the same numbers reflected in the human hands.

This, of course, refers to the positive side of the equation. After we counter the patient's negative energy with negative energy accessed by the healer, we must then dress the patient with the positively charged energy that is unlocked by this heavenly code of 8 and 1. This is the key to unlocking the energy of Paradise, and it is this energy that revives the patient, strengthens him, and cures him.

We see, then, that the entire healing process relies on understanding and activating the heavenly code that is inscribed upon every human hand.   The healer begins by rubbing the hands together, thereby activating the powers of the number nine, opening the channel of complete submission that allows him to become a conduit for Divine Energy, the fiery energy of Hellfire unlocked by the number nineteen. Using this negatively charged energy, the healer attacks the negativity that is the source of illness within the patient's body.   The negatively charged energy dispels that negativity, transforming it into positive energy and leaving the patient with no trace of the negative force. Finally, the healer uses the Divine, Paradise energy unleashed by the heavenly code of 8 and 1 to dress the patient with positive energy and restore health, thereby completing the cure.

OTHER POWERS OF THE HANDS

All of this explains why practitioners of martial arts like *silat* are able to use the hands as weapons, protecting themselves with the power of these Holy Names.   They may not be aware of the physics involved, nor the theological implications, but they know that there is a power there that they are able to tap.   In addition, they know they can use that power to protect themselves and others and to defeat their enemies.   That is because, when God gives, He gives generously and does not take back.

This same power can also be used for healing.   When the Prophet ﷺ healed *Sayyidina* Ali's eye, he opened that reality to him.   That is why— through the energy he had in his hands—he was able to carry the world up to his knees.

… The Prophet said, "Where is Ali bin Abi Talib?" The people replied, "He is suffering from eye trouble, O Apostle of God." He said, "Send for him and bring him to me." So when Ali came, the Prophet put saliva in his eyes and invoked good on him, and he became healthy again as if he had had no ailment…[2]

---

[2] Sahih Bukhari.

SECTION FIVE: CONCLUSION

Each expression of disease is manifested as some form of pain, be it physical, emotional, mental, or spiritual. We have to probe the deeper meanings of our illnesses. "What can we learn from this illness or pain?"

Pain is the bell that drives the body's own self-defense mechanism. It alerts us so that we can correct problems that have developed. Pain is like a warning bell in our system that brings our attention to the fact that something is wrong and forces us do something about it. Pain says, "You are not listening to your whole self." Pain teaches us to ask for help and healing and is, therefore, a key to the education of the soul.

A comprehensive approach to pain relief and health which includes the spiritual dimension of healing will greatly help the progress of modern medicine. Renewed interest in spiritual healing methods will only help to further the state of modern medicine as we benefit from the experiences and knowledge of our predecessors in this noble field. Unfortunately, this topic has too often been dismissed by contemporary physicians, despite the fact that these remedies have been practiced successfully for thousands of years.

Appendix

A

Spiritual Practices

Appendix A

Spiritual Practices & Prayers

DAILY SPIRITUAL PRACTICES FOR INITIATES

ADAB			ادب	
Practice	Dhikr	Arabic	Meaning	Number of times
Bear witness – testimony of faith	ashhadu an la ilaha illal Lah wa ash-hadu anna Muhammadan 'Abduhu wa Rasuluhu	أَشْهَدُ أَنْ لا إله إلا الله وأَشْهَدُ أَنَّ مُحَمَّدًا عَبْدُهُ ورَسُولُهُ	I testify that there is no god but God, and I testify that Muhammad is the Servant and Messenger of God.	3
Seek forgiveness	Astaghfirullah	أَسْتَغْفِرُ الله	God forgive me.	70
Seek blessings	Suratu 'l-Fatiha	الفاتحة الشريفة		1
	Aman ar-rasul (Quran 2:285-6) See below	آمَنَ الرَّسُولُ		1
	Suratu 'l-Ikhlas	سورة الإخلاص		11
	Suratu 'l-Inshirah	سورة الانشراح		7
	Suratu 'l-Falaq	سورة الفلق		1
	Surat un-Nas	سورة الناس		1
Testimony of faith without witnessing (kalimatut-tawhid)	La ilaha illa-Llah	لا إله إلا الله		9

	La ilaha illa-Llah Muhammadun Rasul Allah	لا إله إلا الله مُحَمَّدًا رَسُولُ الله	There is no god but God, and Muhammad ﷺ is the Servant and Messenger of God.	1
Prayers on the Prophet – (salawat)	Allahumma salli 'ala Muhammadin wa 'ala ali Muhammadin wa sallim	اللَّهُمَّ صَلِّ على مُحَمَّدٍ وعلى آلِ مُحَمَّدٍ وسلِّم	O God send blessings and peace upon Muhammad and the family of Muhammad.	10
Gift the reward – Ihda	See below	إهداء		1
Recitation	Suratu 'l-Fatiha	الفاتحة الشريفة		1
WIRD		ورد		
Remember God (dhikr)	Allah, Allah	ذِكْرُ الجلالة: الله الله الله	God, God.	1500
Prayers on the Prophet- (salawat)	Allahumma salli 'ala Muhammadin wa 'ala ali Muhammadin wa sallim	اللَّهُمَّ صَلِّ على مُحَمَّدٍ وعلى آلِ مُحَمَّدٍ وسلِّم	O God send blessings and peace upon Muhammad and the family of Muhammad.	100
Recitation of Quran	One juz' (1/30) of the Quran -or- Suratu 'l-Ikhlas	جزء من القرآن او اخلاص الشريفة		1 -or- 100
Prayers on the Prophet- (salawat)	One chapter of Dala'il al-Khayrat -or- Allahumma salli 'ala Muhammadin wa 'ala ali Muhammadin wa salim	دلائل الخيرات او اللَّهُمَّ صَلِّ على مُحَمَّدٍ وعلى آلِ مُحَمَّدٍ وسلِّم	O God send blessings and peace upon Muhammad ﷺ and the family of Muhammad ﷺ	1 -or- 100

SPIRITUAL PRACTICES FOR THE PREPARED

The Prepared seeker should add the following recitations to what is above:

Increase the number of repetitions of God's name from 1,500 to 2,500 by tongue and add another 2,500 by heart, meditating upon that Name.

Increase the number of prayers on the Prophet ﷺ from 100 to 500 on Monday, Thursday, and Friday, and 300 on the remaining 4 days.

SPIRITUAL PRACTICES FOR PEOPLE OF DETERMINATION

The People of Determination should add the following to the zikr of the Prepared:

The Crown of Prayers on the Prophet ﷺ *(Sayyid as-salawat)* is recited before the Gifting *(Ihda)* (see page 130).

After the *Fatiha* following the Gifting, the seeker repeats *Allah Hu Allah Hu Allah Hu Haqq* three times, imagining himself between the Hands of his Lord.

There is an increase in the number of repetitions of God's Name to 5,000 by tongue and 5,000 by heart, and an increase in the number of prayers on the Prophet ﷺ from 300 to 2,000 on Mondays, Thursdays, and Fridays, and 1,000 on the remaining four days.

Notes Regarding the Spiritual Practices

Prayers

The essence of the practices of the Naqshbandi masters is built on the pillar of prayer and on remembrance of God. For those desiring high stations and distinguished ranks, the observance of prayer is the key. The seekers must strive to imitate their shaykhs in the observance of not only the obligatory prayers, but the supererogatory *sunnah* and *nawafil* prayers that the shaykhs maintain as a constant daily practice. You will find the following practices are based around the five obligatory prayers, in addition to the night vigil, which consists of the Prayer of Safety, the Prayer of Thanks, The Prayer of Praise, and the Night Prayer.

Thus, it is incumbent on the seeker—before attempting the large number of voluntary forms of prayer described in this book—to learn and practice the fundamental principles of the prescribed prayers correctly, based on the prescription of a recognized school of Islamic jurisprudence (choosing from either the *Shafi'i, Maliki, Hanbali* or *Hanafi* schools). These include purification from greater or lesser impurities—the greater ablution or the lesser ablution; proper intention; facing the *qiblah* determined according to the principles of the school of jurisprudence that you follow, and, where possible, praying in congregation. Additionally, the integrals of the prayers should be observed correctly, including the proper movements, for the Prophet ﷺ said, "There is no prayer for one who does not straighten his back in bowing and prostration." Thus the new seeker in this Way, if not already acquainted and familiar with these fundamentals, must seek out an authorized teacher and learn them.

Testimony of Faith

The Testimony of Faith is pronounced three times. The first is for his own self, bringing to mind the Presence of the Prophet ﷺ and saying in one's heart, "O my master; O Prophet of God! You are my witness; God is my witness; all angels, Companions, and prophets are my witnesses; everyone in creation is my witnesses; and my shaykh is my witness," then pronounce the testimony, for you are renewing your Islam. Then pronounce the second testimony on behalf of yourself, your parents, your children, your family, your brothers and sisters, your relations, your friends and neighbors, and all Muslim people. The third testimony is said on behalf of unbelievers with the intention that they become believers.

ALLAHU…ALLAHU…ALLAHU…HAQQ

Sit on your knees, meditating on the connection to your shaykh, from your shaykh to the Prophet ﷺ, and from the Prophet ﷺ to the Divine Presence.

THE VERSE "THE MESSENGER BELIEVETH…" (2:285-286)

AYAT AMAN AR-RASUL (2:285-286)	آمَنَ الرَّسُولُ
Āmana ar-rasūlu bimā unzila ilayhi min Rabbihi wa 'l-mu'minūn. kullun āmana Billāhi wa malā'ikatihi wa kutubihi wa rusulihi lā nufarriqu bayna āhadin min rusulihi wa qālū sam'inā wa atanā ghufrānaka Rabbanā wa ilaykal maṣīr. lā yukallif-Ullāhu nafsan illa wus'ahā. lahā mā kasabat wa 'alayhā māktasabat. Rabbanā lā tū'ākhidhnā in nasīnā aw akhṭānā. Rabbanā wa lā taḥmil 'alaynā iṣran kamā ḥamaltahu 'alā alladhīnā min qablinā. Rabbanā wa lā tuḥamilnā mā lā ṭāqata lanā bihi w'afu 'anā waghfir lanā warḥamnā Anta Mawlānā f'anṣurnā 'alā l-qawm il-kāfirīn.	آمَنَ الرَّسُولُ بِمَا أُنزِلَ إِلَيْهِ مِن رَّبِّهِ وَالْمُؤْمِنُونَ كُلٌّ آمَنَ بِاللّهِ وَمَلآئِكَتِهِ وَكُتُبِهِ وَرُسُلِهِ لاَ نُفَرِّقُ بَيْنَ أَحَدٍ مِّن رُّسُلِهِ وَقَالُوا سَمِعْنَا وَأَطَعْنَا غُفْرَانَكَ رَبَّنَا وَإِلَيْكَ الْمَصِيرُ لاَ يُكَلِّفُ اللّهُ نَفْسًا إِلاَّ وُسْعَهَا لَهَا مَا كَسَبَتْ وَعَلَيْهَا مَا اكْتَسَبَتْ رَبَّنَا لاَ تُؤَاخِذْنَا إِن نَّسِينَا أَوْ أَخْطَأْنَا رَبَّنَا وَلاَ تَحْمِلْ عَلَيْنَا إِصْرًا كَمَا حَمَلْتَهُ عَلَى الَّذِينَ مِن قَبْلِنَا رَبَّنَا وَلاَ تُحَمِّلْنَا مَا لاَ طَاقَةَ لَنَا بِهِ وَاعْفُ عَنَّا وَاغْفِرْ لَنَا وَارْحَمْنَا أَنتَ مَوْلاَنَا فَانصُرْنَا عَلَى الْقَوْمِ الْكَافِرِينَ

The Messenger believeth in what hath been revealed to him from his Lord, as do the men of faith. Each one (of them) believeth in God, His angels, His books, and His apostles. "We make no distinction (they say) between one and another of His apostles." And they say: "We hear, and we obey: (We seek) Thy forgiveness, our Lord, and to Thee is the end of all journeys." On no soul doth God place a burden greater than it can bear. It gets every good that it earns, and it suffers every ill that it earns. (Pray:) "Our Lord! Condemn us not if we

> forget or fall into error; our Lord! Lay not on us a burden like that which Thou didst lay on those before us; Our Lord! Lay not on us a burden greater than we have strength to bear. Blot out our sins, and grant us forgiveness. Have mercy on us. Thou art our Protector; Help us against those who stand against faith."

Whoever recites this verse will attain a high rank and a great position. He will receive the station of safety in this world and the next. He will enter the circle of security in the Presence of God, Almighty and Exalted. He will reach all the stations of the most distinguished Naqshbandi Order. He will be an inheritor of the secret of the Prophet ﷺ and of the saints, and will arrive at the stage of Bayazid al-Bistami ق, the Imam of the Order, who said, "I am also the Truth." This is the magnificent manifestation which belongs to this verse, and to other verses also. Grandshaykh Khalid al-Baghdadi ق received the vision and the secret of this verse, through which God made him special for his time.

Suratu 'l-Fatiha (1)

The first time Suratu 'l-Fatiha is recited, it is with the intention of participating in the blessings sent down with it when it was revealed in Makkah. The second time it is recited should be with the intention of sharing in the Divine Grace which was sent down when it was revealed the second time in Madina. Grandshaykh said, "If someone recites Suratu 'l-Fatiha, he will not leave this world without attaining those Divine Blessings that are hidden behind the meaning of Suratu 'l-Fatiha which enable him to reach a state of submission to God, Almighty and Exalted."

The blessings that God has sent down with Suratu 'l-Fatiha when it was revealed to the Prophet ﷺ will never cease, and will last forever with the one who recites Suratu 'l-Fatiha. No one is able to know how much blessings there are except God and His Messenger ﷺ. Whoever recites it without this intention receives general Divine Favors, while whoever recites Suratu 'l-Fatiha, with the intention of sharing in the Divine Grace will attain a high position and a great rank. This *Surah* possesses innumerable and limitless stations in the Sight of God, Who is Powerful and Sublime.

THE CROWN OF PRAYERS ON THE PROPHET ﷺ

Sayyid as-Salawat	سَيّدُ الصَّلاةِ الشَّرِيفَةِ المَأثُورَة
'alā ashraf il-'ālamīna Sayyidinā Muhammadini salawāt ﷺ. 'alā afḍal il-'ālamīna Sayyidinā Muhammadini salawāt ﷺ. 'alā akmal il-'ālamīna Sayyidinā Muhammadini salawāt ﷺ.	على أَشْرَفِ العالَمِينَ سَيّدِنا مُحَمَّدٍ الصَّلَوات. على أَفْضَلِ العالَمِينَ سَيّدِنا مُحَمَّدٍ الصَّلَوات. على أَكْمَلِ العالَمِينَ سَيّدِنا مُحَمَّدٍ الصَّلَوات.
Ṣalawātullāhi ta'ālā wa malā'ikatihi wa anbiyā'ihī wa rusulihi wa jamī'i khalqihi 'alā Muhammadin wa 'alā āli Muhammad, 'alayhi wa 'alayhimu 's-salām wa rahmatullāhi ta'ālā wa barakātuhu, wa raḍī-Allāhū tabāraka wa ta'ālā 'an sādātinā ashābi Rasūlillāhi ajma'īn, wa 'an it-tab'īna bihim bi ihsān, wa 'an il-a'immat il-mujtahidīn al-māḍīn, wa 'an il-'ulamā il-muttaqqīn, wa 'an il-awliyā 'iṣ-ṣāliḥīn, wa 'ām-mashayikhinā fit-ṭarīqati 'n-Naqshbandīyyati 'l-'alīyya, qaddas-Allāhū ta'ālā arwāḥahum uz-zakīyya, wa nawwar Allāhū ta'ālā aḍriḥatahumu 'l-mubāraka, wa a'ād-Allāhū ta'ālā 'alaynā min barakātihim wa fuyūḍātihim dā'iman wa 'l-ḥamdulillāhi Rabb il-'alamīn, al-Fātiḥā.	صَلَواتُ اللهِ تَعالى ومَلائِكَتِهِ وأَنْبِيائِهِ ورُسُلِهِ وجَميعِ خَلْقِهِ على مُحَمَّدٍ وعلى آلِ مُحَمَّدٍ، عليه وعليهِمُ السَّلامُ ورَحْمَةُ اللهِ تَعالى وبَرَكاتُهُ ورَضِيَ اللهُ تَبارَكَ وتَعالى عَنْ سادَتِنا أَصْحابِ رَسُولِ اللهِ أَجْمَعينَ وعَنِ التَّابِعينَ لهم بإِحْسانٍ وعَنِ الأَئِمَّةِ المُجْتَهِدِينَ الماضِينَ وعَنِ العُلَماءِ المُتَّقِينَ وعَنِ الأَوْلِياءِ الصَّالِحينَ وعَنْ مَشايِخِنا في الطَّرِيقَةِ النَّقْشْبَنْدِيَّةِ العَلِيَّةِ، قَدَّسَ اللهُ تَعالى أَرْواحَهُمُ الزَّكِيَّة وَوَرَّ اللهُ تَعالى أَضْرِحَتَهُمُ المُبارَكَة وأَعادَ اللهُ تَعالى عَلينا مِنْ بَرَكاتِهِمْ وفُيُوضاتِهِمْ دائِمًا والحَمْدُ للهِ رَبِّ العالَمِينَ —الفاتِحَة

Upon the Noblest of all Creation, our Master Muhammad, blessings.

Upon the most Preferred of all Creation, our Master Muhammad, blessings.

Upon the most Perfect of all Creation, our Master Muhammad, blessings.

Blessings of God (Exalted is He!), of His angels, of His prophets, of His Emissaries, and of all creation be upon Muhammad ﷺ and the family of Muhammad ﷺ; may the peace and mercy of God (Exalted is He!) and His blessings be upon him and upon them. May God, the Blessed and Most High, be pleased with every one of our Masters, the Companions of the Emissary of God, and with those who followed them in excellence, and with the early masters of juristic reasoning, and with the pious scholars, and the righteous saints and with our shaykhs in the exalted Naqshbandi Order. May God (Exalted is He!) sanctify their pure souls, and illuminate their blessed graves. May God (Exalted is He!) return to us of their blessings and overflowing bounty, always. Praise belongs to God, the Lord of the worlds, al-Fatiha.

DEDICATION

GIFTING (*IHDA*)	إهداء
Allāhumma balligh thawāba mā qarā'nāhū wa nūra mā talawnāhū hadīyyatan wāṣilatan minnā ila rūḥi Nabīyyīnā Sayyidinā wa Mawlānā Muḥammadin ṣalla-llāhū 'alayhi wa sallam. Wa ilā arwāḥi ikhwānihi min al-anbiyā'i wa 'l-mursalīn wa khudamā'i sharā'ihim wa ila arwāḥi al-a'immati al-arba' wa ila arwāḥi mashaykhinā fiṭ-ṭarīqati an-naqshbandīyyati al-'aliyyati khāṣṣatan ila rūḥi Imām aṭ-ṭarīqati wa ghawth il-khalīqati Khāja Bahāuddīn an-Naqshband Muḥammad al-Uwaisī al-Bukhārī wa ḥaḍarati ustādhinā Mawlanā Sulṭān al-awlīyā Shaykhunā ash-Shaykh 'Abd Allāh al-Fā'iz ad-Dāghestanī wa sayyidunā ash-Shaykh Muḥammad Nāẓim al-Ḥaqqānī Mu'ayyad ad-dīn wa sa'iri sādātinā waṣ-ṣiddiqiyyīna al-Fātiḥā.	اللَّهُمَّ بَلِّغْ ثَوَابَ ما قرأناهُ ونورَ ما تلونَاهُ هَدِيَّةً واصِلَةً مِنَّا إلى روح نبينا مُحَمَّد (صلى الله عليه وسلم وإلى أرواح إخوانه من الأنبياء والمرسلين وخُدَماءِ شَرائعهم وإلى أرواح الأئمّة الأربعة وإلى أرواح مشايخنا في الطريقة النقشبندية العَلِيَّة، خاصة إلى روح إمام الطريقة وغوث الخليقة خواجه بهاء الدين النقشبند مُحَمَّد الأويسي البخاري وإلى مَوْلانا سُلطان الأولياء الشَّيخ عَبْد الله الفائز الداغِسْتاني وإلى مولانا سيدنا الشيخ محمد ناظم الحقّاني مؤيد الدين الدين والصدّقين الفاتحة

O God! Grant that the merit of what we have read, and the light of what we have recited, are (considered) an offering and gift from us to the soul of our Prophet Muhammad, and to the souls of the prophets, and the saints; in particular the soul of the Imam of the tariqat and arch-Intercessor of the created world, Khwaja Bahauddin an-Naqshband Muhammad al-Uwaisi al-Bukhari, and our venerable teacher and master, the Sultan of Saints, our Shaykh Abdullah ad-Daghestani, and our master Shaykh Muhammad Nazim al-Haqqani Mu'ayyad ad-din, and to all our masters and to the righteous... al-Fatiha.

This presents the reward of the preceding recitations to the Prophet ﷺ and to the shaykhs of the Naqshbandi Order.

SURATUL-IKHLAS (112)

Whoever recites this *Surah* should obtain the Divine Grace of the two Names of Glory, the One (*al-Ahad*), and the Eternal *(as-Samad)*. Anyone who reads it must receive a portion of this.

SURATUL-INSHIRAH (94)

On each letter and on each verse of the Quran there is a Divine manifestation, which is different from that on any other. Whoever recites a verse or letter of the Quran will attain the Divine Grace that is particular to that verse or letter. If anyone recites this *Surah* of the Quran, he will receive that Divine Grace and those virtues. Whoever wishes to obtain these virtues, must keep these spiritual practices daily along with his obligations. Then he will gain true and eternal life.

SURATUL-FALAQ (113) AND SURATUN-NAS (114)

The reality of the secret and the perfect wholeness of God's Greatest Name are connected with these two chapters. Since they mark the end of the Quran, they are linked with the completion of the Divine Grace. By means of these spiritual practices, the masters of the most distinguished Naqshbandi Order became oceans of knowledge and gnosis. Grandshaykh Abdullah ad-Daghestani said:

> You have now reached the beginning, where each verse, letter and Surah of the Quran has its own special manifestation which does not resemble any other. For that reason the Messenger of God 襁 said, *"I left three things with my Community—death which makes them afraid, true dreams which give them good tidings, and the Quran which speaks to them."* By means of the Quran, God will open up the gates of Divine Grace in the Last Times, as it came down in the time of the Holy Prophet 襁 and the Companions, and in the times of the caliphs, and in the time of the saints.

> These stations and continuous Divine Graces are closely bound together and cannot be separated, so any deficiency in the spiritual

practices will automatically create a deficiency in the Divine Grace being sent down. As an example, if we want to wash our hands, we may wait in front of the tap for water to come out. If the pipes are disconnected so that the water escapes before reaching the tap, then no matter how long we wait, the water will not flow out. So we must not let any deficiency enter our *dhikr* until we obtain the Divine Grace.

These spiritual practices for the three different levels of followers must be performed once every twenty-four hours, together with all other obligations, according to the Divine Law. Everything which the Prophet ﷺ brought was founded on these spiritual practices. It is the way that the servant reaches the key of Nearness to God, the All-Powerful, the Sublime. It was by means of it that the prophets, messengers, and saints reached their Creator, and it is by means of these spiritual practices that we reach all these stations of the most distinguished Order.

The masters of the most distinguished Naqshbandi Order say that whoever claims that he is affiliated with one of the other orders or with the most distinguished Naqshbandi Order, but nevertheless has not entered seclusion even once in his life, then such a person should be ashamed of connecting himself with the people of the path.

In our time, Grandshaykh Abdullah ad-Daghestani ق said:

Whoever of the people of the end of time wishes to attain a high rank and an exalted state and receive what a disciple normally receives by means of seclusion and spiritual exercises must continuously perform these spiritual practices and remembrances of God. With these as the foundation, we have set the way for the higher stations—they are built on this foundation. The disciple ought to know that if he fails to attain an exalted station and high grade in this world because of his lack of effort, then he shall not be separated from this world, but that the shaykhs make him reach it, and reveal for him his station, either during his lifetime, or at the time of the seven last breaths during the agonies of death.

If anyone performs these spiritual practices and then performs an action which is forbidden, he will be like the one who builds his house on the side of a cliff, and then his house collapses down the side of the cliff. So we should always be aware of our actions, gauging them to see if they are permitted or forbidden, if God is going to be angry with our actions or not. And we need to think about every action so much that ultimately we do not do any unlawful thing which might weaken our foundation. As the Prophet ﷺ said in his Tradition, *"One hour's contemplation is better than seventy years of worship."* We should perform our actions in the perfectly correct way, that is to say without any prohibited deeds intervening.

On this basis, God has divided the day into three parts: eight hours for worship, eight hours for earning a living, and eight hours for sleeping. Anyone who does not accept and follow this division of energies will exemplify the Tradition, "He who is erratic will be erratic in the Hellfire." He who goes according to his own will and reasoning does not progress, and he who wishes to obtain exalted stations, levels, and stages which previous generations earned by means of retreats and other spiritual exercises must remember God throughout the course of the day.

He who makes a regular practice of these spiritual exercises shall attain the Water of True Life, with which he will perform ablution. He will bathe in it, and drink it, and by means of it he shall reach his goal. There may be a person who claims that he has been in the Order for thirty years and as yet has not seen anything and not attained anything. That person should look at his actions over the past years. How many deficient actions has he performed? When he sees the deficiency he should quickly avoid it, then he will reach God, Who is Powerful and Sublime. When the disciple forsakes the daily duties which the shaykhs have told him to perform, then he will be absolutely incapable of making further progress, and he will be unable to keep any state he had previously attained. No prophet ever attained prophethood, nor did any saint ever attain sainthood, nor did any believer ever attain the stage of faith without utilizing his time for his daily *dhikr*.

Verses and Traditions of Prophet Muhammad
Regarding Meditation (Tafakkur)

Appendix B

Verses and Traditions of Prophet Muhammad Regarding Meditation (Tafakkur)

*T*he Prophet of God ﷺ said:

> A caller will call on the Day of Judgment, "Where are people of understanding? They would answer, "Which of those you seek?" The caller said, *"Those who remember God standing sitting and lying down on their sides; and they reflect upon the creation of heavens and earth saying: O our Lord You have not created all this in vain; praise be to You and save us from the punishment of fire.*[1] Those have been given a flag and people will follow their flag, and it will be said on to them 'enter it (heaven) for eternity.'"[2]

The Prophet of God ﷺ came upon his companions while they were meditating, so he said to them:

> Do not meditate upon God; rather meditate upon His creation.[3]

The Prophet ﷺ said:

> Reflect upon anything except God's Essence.[4]

'Amir bin Abd Kais ؓ said, "I heard this from more than one, two or three companions, 'the light or glow of faith is meditation.'"[5]

Ibn Aun related:

---

[1] Surat Ali-'Imran, 3:191.

[2] Al-Asbahani related in his *at-Targhib* from Abu Hurayrah.

[3] Ibn Abi Hatim and Al-Asbahani in his *at-Targhib* from Abdullah ibn Salam.

[4] Ibn Abi Hatim and Al-Bayhaqi, related in "*Al-Asma'a wa 's-sifat*" (*The Divine Names and Attributes*) that from Ibn 'Abbas.

[5] Ibn Abi 'd-Dunya from 'Amir bin Abd Kais.

I asked Umm 'd-Darda ❀ (wife of the companion Abu 'd-Darda ❀), what Abu 'd-Darda's preferred form of worship was. She ❀ said, "Meditation and reflection."[6]

Ibn 'Abbas ❀ said, "Meditation for one hour is better than standing the night in prayer."[7]

Anas ❀ said, "Meditation upon the difference between night and day is better the worship of eighty years." [8]

The Prophet of God ❀ said, "The meditation of one hour is better than the worship of sixty years."[9]

It is related in the *Mathni* that according to Isma'il, he said: I heard Aba Salmah bin 'Abd ar-Rahman comment on the recitation by my father on the verse:

As if it was not prosperous yesterday,[10]

[means] "We would not have destroyed it had it not been for the sins of its inhabitants."

Regarding (the succeeding line in the verse):

In this manner do We explain the signs for people who reflect. [11]

He said that it means, "In the same manner We have taught you about the material world and showed you its laws and affairs, We will show you our proofs and evidence for those who meditate, reflect and study."

---

[6] Ibn Sa'ad, Ibn Abi Shaibah , Ahmad in *az-Zuhd* along with Ibn al-Mundhir.

[7] Al-Qurtubi.

[8] Ad-Daylami.

[9] Abu ash-Shaykh related in *al-'Adhamah* from Abu Hurayrah.

[10] Surah Yunus, 10:24

[11] Surah Yunus, 10:24

He specifically mentioned the people of reflection, because they are the people of discerning between the different matters, and who search for the realities of things which are obscure.[12]

Regarding the interpretation of God's words:

God overtakes the souls when they die, and the ones which did not die while sleeping; he holds back the one which death have overtaken, as for the one which did not die He sends back for a decreed period...

And His words:

In this there are signs for those who reflect. [13]

God is saying that by His withholding of the souls of the dead and of those asleep, and that by His sending the souls of those sleeping, back to their bodies, while keeping the other souls which died from going back to their bodies: He is giving an example and a lesson to those who reflect and search. It is proof for them that God gives life to whomever he chooses from his creation, and chooses death for whomever He wants.

Another verse is:

They reflect upon the creation of the heavens and the earth.[14]

We have elaborated upon the meaning of remembering (yadhkurun) which is done either by tongue or by praying obligatory and voluntary prayers. But He (God) added another form of devotion to the one mentioned, which is to reflect upon the power of God, His creation and the lessons He gives, in order for their inner eye to open:

---

[12] In the Mathni narrated from Ishaq, from Abu Usamah.
[13] Suratu's-Zumar, 39:42.
[14] Surat Ali-'Imran, 3:191.

In every thing He has a sign

Which proves that He is One [15]

The Prophet ﷺ passed by some people who were meditating upon God, so he said:

Meditate upon the creation and do not meditate upon The Creator, because you can not make a just estimate of Him.

Therefore meditation, reflection, and the widening of horizons, can only be applied to creation...

It was said that Sufyan ath-Thawri prayed two cycles behind the Station of Prophet Abraham ﷺ, and then he raised his head up towards the sky. When he saw the planets he passed out. He used to urinate blood due to his being sad and his meditating for a long time.

It was narrated by Abu Hurayrah ﷺ, that the Prophet of God ﷺ said:

While lying down on his bed, a man raised up his head and looked at the stars, saying, "I bear witness that you have a lord and a creator. O my Lord, forgive me." So God looked upon him and forgave him.[16]

It is also related:

There is no worship like meditation.

Umm 'd-Darda ﷺ was asked, "What was the worship which Abu 'd-Darda ﷺ practiced most?" She said it was meditation. [So] they asked Abu 'd-Darda, "Do you see meditation as a deed amongst other (devotional) deeds?" He said, "Yes, it is certainty (*al-yaqeen*)."[17]

[15] Surah Yunus, 10:24.
[16] Abu ash-Shaykh and ad-Daylami.

Ibn Abbas, Abu 'd-Darda and Al-Hasan ﷺ said, "Meditation is the mirror for the believer; in it he can see his good and bad deeds"[18]

It is related:

One night while hosting a guest, Abu Sulayman ad-Darrani carried a jug of water on his way to make ablution for the night prayers. The guest saw that as soon as Abu Sulayman put his fingers through the ear of the jug, he sat down meditating until the dawn prayer. So he asked him "What happened O Abu Sulayman?" He said, "As soon as I put my fingers through the ear of the jug, I started reflecting upon the verse:

"When the yokes (shall be) round their necks, and the chains; they shall be dragged along."[19]

So I meditated upon myself and about how I would receive the shackle when it is thrown around my neck on the Day of Judgment, I was engrossed like this till morning.

Ibn 'Arabi said:

The scholars of Muslims differed on the question of whether prayer is better than meditation. The Sufis said that meditation is better, because its fruit is knowledge, and this is best amongst the legal stations.

Ibn 'Abbas ﷺ related that one night he slept over at his aunt Maimuna's (the wife of the Prophet ﷺ) house. At night the Prophet awakened and wiped sleep off his face and then recited the last ten verses from Surat Aali 'Imran. He then got up and made a light ablution and then prayed thirteen cycles.

---

[17] Imam Malik from Ibn al-Qassim.

[18] Al-Qurtubi.

[19] Surah Ghafir,40:71.

Look therefore at how he combined between reflecting upon creation, and prayer.[20]

Notes

Notes

Notes

Notes

Notes

Notes

Notes

Notes

Notes

Notes

Notes

Notes

Printed in the United Kingdom
by Lightning Source UK Ltd.
106570UKS00003B/137